SECOND EDITION

Pronunciation Pairs

An Introduction to the Sounds of English

ANN BAKER

SHARON GOLDSTEIN

CAMBRIDGE
UNIVERSITY PRESS

CAMBRIDGE UNIVERSITY PRESS
Cambridge, New York, Melbourne, Madrid, Cape Town,
Singapore, São Paulo, Delhi, Mexico City

Cambridge University Press
32 Avenue of the Americas, New York, NY 10013–2473, USA

www.cambridge.org
Information on this title: www.cambridge.org/9780521678087

First published 1990
Second edition 2008
9th printing 2013

Printed in the United States of America

A catalogue record for this publication is available from the British Library.

Library of Congress Cataloging-in-Publication Data

Baker, Ann.
   Pronunciation pairs : an introduction to the sounds of English / Ann Baker. -- 2nd ed.
       p. cm.
   Rev. of: 1st ed., 1990.
   Summary: "The Pronunciation Pairs, Second Edition, Student's Book has updated dialogs, which include
current and useful vocabulary. Hundreds of simple, clear illustrations help students understand the dialogs
and vocabulary. An audio CD with selections from the complete class audio program is included in the back
of the Student's Book" "--Provided by publisher.
   ISBN 978-0-521-67808-7 (student's book)
1. English language--Pronunciation by foreign speakers. 2. English language--Textbooks for foreign speakers.
I. Goldstein, Sharon. II. Title.

       PE1137.B215 2007
       428.3'4--dc22

2007025850

ISBN 978-0-521-67808-7 Student's Book
ISBN 978-0-521-67809-4 Teacher's Manual
ISBN 978-0-521-67811-7 Class Audio CDs
ISBN 978-0-521-67810-0 Class Audio Cassettes

Art direction and book design: Adventure House, NYC
Cover design: Adventure House, NYC
Layout: TSI Graphic Services
Audio production: Richard LePage and Associates

Contents

Section A • Vowels

Section B • Consonants

To the Teacher

Pronunciation Pairs, Second Edition, is designed to help high beginning to intermediate students recognize and produce the sounds of North American English. It covers all the vowel and consonant sounds of the language, as well as stress, rhythm, intonation, linking, and other features of connected speech. The book can be used in the classroom, in a language lab, or for self-study.

The 50 units may be taught in whatever order seems most useful. You may want to work through the units in sequence, alternate vowel and consonant units, or choose only the units that are helpful for your students' particular pronunciation difficulties. A diagnostic test to help identify those difficulties appears in the Teacher's Manual.

New Features of the Second Edition

Changes from the first edition of *Pronunciation Pairs* include:
- More active listening tasks
- More interactive speaking tasks
- Updated dialogs with related practice tasks
- Practice of stress, rhythm, intonation, or other features of connected speech in every unit
- Lists of common expressions for each target sound
- More realistic mouth illustrations and detailed directions for producing sounds
- Review units for both the vowel and consonant sections
- All new illustrations and two-color design
- Updated illustrations and two-color interior design
- Free audio CD in the Student's Book, with excerpts from the class audio program
- Free Web site for extra practice and reference

Organization of the Student's Book

Pronunciation Pairs is divided into two sections – one on vowels and one on consonants. Each section begins with an introductory unit that shows the basic mouth positions and movements needed to produce the sounds in that section. After the introductory unit, each unit presents a specific sound through a variety of tasks. The tasks move from highly structured practice of the target sound in individual words to more communicative practice of the sound in connected speech, including guided conversations, games, puzzles, and interactive speaking tasks. There are also eight review units.

The units in the Student's Book generally follow this format:
- **Mouth illustrations and directions.** Each unit begins with an illustration of the position of the tongue and other parts of the mouth for the target sound. The illustration is accompanied by directions for making the sound.

- **Word pairs**. Illustrated word pairs appear in almost every unit. Word pairs (also known as *minimal pairs*) are pairs of words, like *ship* and *sheep*, that differ by only one sound. Each set of word pairs contrasts the target sound with another very similar sound. The words are illustrated to make the difference in meaning clear. Making it visually obvious that changing a single sound in a word can completely alter the meaning helps students understand the importance of accurate pronunciation.

- **Sound recognition tests.** Every unit that presents illustrated word pairs then tests students' ability to distinguish between the sounds being contrasted, first in isolated words and then within sentences. This gives students practice in hearing and identifying the target sound in connected speech.

- **Vocabulary.** Each unit includes a list of words or phrases containing the target sound. The vocabulary words prepare students for the dialog and tasks that follow. An attempt has been made throughout to use simple, everyday words.

- **Dialog.** Each unit contains a dialog or other listening selection with a high concentration of the sound (or sounds) being practiced in the unit. The dialogs are written to sound as natural as possible, and students do not need to understand every word. Each dialog includes a guided listening task that involves use of the target sound.

- **Stress, rhythm, and intonation.** In addition to practicing a particular sound, each unit practices stress, rhythm, intonation, or some other feature of connected speech. The unit subtitle highlights this feature.

- **Practice activities.** Every unit includes one or more interactive speaking tasks, including games, role plays, guided conversations, discussions, or surveys that practice both the target sound and the feature of connected speech presented in the unit.

- **Spelling.** Each unit includes a spelling section that lists the basic spelling patterns for the sound being practiced, using words from the unit as examples.

- **Common expressions.** Each unit concludes with a summary of common phrases and sentences that contain the sound taught in the unit. Practicing these expressions can help improve fluency and encourage students to use the target sound outside the classroom.

Components of the Second Edition

- **Student's Book** packaged with an audio CD that includes material excerpted from the class audio program

- **Classroom audio program**, available on five audio CDs or cassettes, that contains all the examples and practice material marked with the 🎧 symbol in the Student's Book

- **Teacher's Manual** that provides additional help and guidance for teachers using the Student's Book in their classes, answers to all tasks, notes on student difficulties, activities for further practice, and suggestions for linking pronunciation lessons with other coursework

- **Free Web site** (www.cambridge.org/pp/student) with additional practice material for each unit of the Student's Book, a chart of the IPA sound symbols, and a List of Likely Errors that gives information on the difficulties speakers of different languages are likely to have

To the Student

Pronunciation Pairs, Second Edition, will help you recognize and pronounce all the vowel and consonant sounds of North American English. Each unit practices a different sound or reviews a group of sounds. Each unit also practices a speech feature such as stress, intonation, rhythm, or linking words together. These features are as important as individual sounds for speaking and understanding English.

There are many types of listening and speaking activities in the book. Most of the units include word pairs that contrast two sounds. Word pairs are pairs of words, such as *night* and *light*, that are the same except for one sound. If your first language does not have one or both of the different sounds in the word pair, practicing the word pairs can help you learn to hear – and produce – the two different sounds.

Pronunciation Pairs has two main sections – one on vowels and one on consonants. Each section has an introduction to making the sounds in that section. You can work through the book from beginning to end or you can choose units that practice the sounds or other pronunciation features that are difficult for you.

In each unit, a vocabulary list gives you practice saying the sound in everyday words, and a spelling section shows you how the sound is spelled. A dialog or other listening selection gives you practice in hearing the sound in conversation. You will also have the opportunity to practice the sound with other students in conversations, games, or other activities. Each unit ends with a list of some common words and sentences that use the sound. Practicing these expressions can help you improve your fluency and remind you when to use the sound outside the classroom.

You can use this book in a class with a teacher or in a language lab. You can also use many of the tasks for self-study. If you are using the book for self study, find a partner to practice the conversations, games, or other activities. An audio CD is included at the back of your book. This audio CD has some of the material from the full class audio program. A list of the material recorded on this CD is shown on the inside back cover.

You will find the following equipment helpful:

• a CD player or computer for listening to the recordings on the Student's Book audio CD
• equipment for recording your own voice
• a mirror for comparing the position of your mouth with the pictures of the mouth in each unit

You can find extra practice for each unit on the Web site for *Pronunciation Pairs* at www.cambridge.org/pp/student

Acknowledgments

*P*ronunciation Pairs, Second Edition, is based on the British text *Ship* or *Sheep?* by Ann Baker.

Many people contributed to the new edition. Thanks are particularly owed to:

The reviewers Ruth Chavez, Leslie Neal, Sarah Plews, Ruth Wagner, and Duncan White, who used and commented on the first edition of *Pronunciation Pairs*. Their suggestions were very helpful in developing the second edition.

The design team at Adventure House, including Jason Fortuna, Rachel Smith, and Jamey O'Quinn, who are responsible for the eye-catching look of this new edition.

The illustrators, Adam Hurwitz, who skillfully rendered all the mouth diagrams, and William Waitzman, who worked tirelessly to produce the hundreds of illustrations.

Mary Sandre, the Web site developer, and Kimley Maretzo, the Web site designer, who created the *Pronunciation Pairs* Web site.

Richard LePage, for his keen ear and professionalism in producing the audio program.

Jane Mairs, the commissioning editor, who initiated and expertly supervised the project. Danielle Powers, Cindee Howard, and particularly Brigit Dermott, the senior project editors who ably guided the book through production.

Thanks, especially, to my development editor, Karen McAlister Shimoda, for her unfailing patience, meticulous attention to detail, and astute advice.

And thanks to Jim and Louisa, who helped me in more ways than they know.

Section A
VOWELS

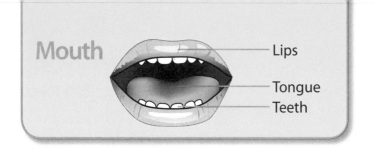

Mouth
Lips
Tongue
Teeth

Making

Practice moving your mouth.

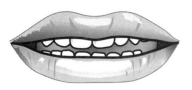 

1. Open your mouth a little bit.

2. Open your mouth a little more.

3. Open your mouth wide.

Practice moving your tongue.

 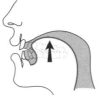 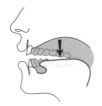 

1. Push your tongue forward.

2. Pull your tongue back.

3. Move your tongue up.

4. Put your tongue down.

5. Curl the tip of your tongue up and back.

Practice making tense and relaxed vowel sounds.

The muscles of the mouth are tense for some vowel sounds and relaxed for others.

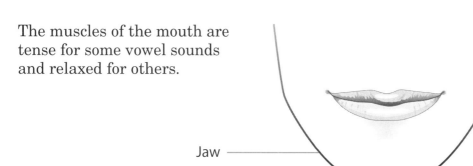

Jaw

1. Push your tongue forward and up.

Spread your lips into a smile.

Put your hand under your jaw.

Practice the sound /iy/: easy, see, tea.

Your muscles should feel tight – or tense.

Vowel Sounds

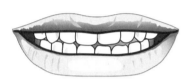

4. Spread your lips into a smile.

5. Make your lips a little round.

6. Push your lips forward into a tight circle.

The pictures to the right show how to make the sounds /iy/ (as in *tea*), /ɑ/ (as in *father* or *hot*), and /uw/ (as in *too*).

Feel how your tongue moves as you say /iy/, /ɑ/, and /uw/.

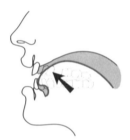

1. Push your tongue forward and up: /iy/

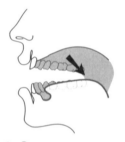

2. Put your tongue down and back.

   Open your mouth wide: /ɑ/

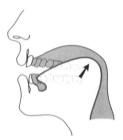

3. Pull your tongue up and back: /uw/

2. Pull your tongue up and back.

   Push your lips forward into a tight circle.

   Put your hand under your jaw.

   Practice the sound /uw/: too, school, who.

   Your muscles should feel tight – or tense.

3. Let your tongue rest in the middle of your mouth.

   Let your mouth rest open.

   Put your hand under your jaw.

   Practice the sound /ʌ/: cup, bus, uh.

   Your muscles should feel relaxed.

/iy/ • tea

Stressed Syllables in Words

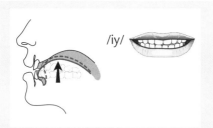

🎧 Open your mouth just a little for the sound /iy/.
Spread your lips into a smile.
Push your tongue forward in your mouth.
/iy/ is a long sound.
Move your tongue up a little as you say it.
Listen and repeat: /iy/.

A Vocabulary

🎧 **1** The sound /iy/ is very long in these words. Listen and repeat.

| tea | three | cheese |

| bean | meal |

🎧 **2** The sound /iy/ is shorter in these words. Listen and repeat.

| meat | peach | Greek |

| pizza | coffee |

3 Is the /iy/ sound longer in the words on the left or the words on the right? Listen and repeat.

see	eat
please	beef
cream	complete

B Dialog: Eating out

Three friends are at a pizza restaurant.

PETE'S PIZZA
MENU

Complete Meal Only $15

Bean Soup *or* Greek Salad
Three Cheese Pizza *or* Meat Pizza (beef and pepperoni)
Ice Cream *or* Cheesecake *or* Peaches (in season)
Coffee *or* Tea

---

1 Cover the dialog and listen. Circle the correct words in parentheses.

1. Steve doesn't eat (cheese / meat / beans).
2. They order (two cheese pizzas and one meat pizza /
   two meat pizzas and one cheese pizza).
3. Three people order (Greek salad / coffee).

2 Listen again and read the dialog. Check your answers to step **1**.

Deena	What are you getting to eat, Lee?
Lee	The meat pizza and Greek salad. And a cup of coffee.
Deena	Me, too. Are you getting the meat pizza, too, Steve?
Steve	No, the cheese pizza. I don't eat meat.
Lee	Really?
Waitress	Good evening. Are you ready to order?
Deena	Let's see . . . We'd like two meat pizzas and one cheese pizza.
Waitress	Bean soup or Greek salad to start?
All three	Greek salad.
Waitress	And would you like coffee or tea?
Deena	Three coffees, please.
Steve	Make that two coffees. Tea for me, please.
Waitress	(*repeating the order*) Three Greek salads . . . two meat pizzas . . . one cheese pizza . . . two coffees . . . one tea.

C Stressed Syllables in Words

- A syllable is a part of a word. Each syllable has a vowel sound.
- *Cheese* has one syllable; *piz • za* has two syllables; *cheese • bur • ger* has three syllables.
- In English words with more than one syllable, one syllable is **stressed**, or stronger. The stressed syllable sounds **louder** and s l o w e r.
- Some English words with two syllables have stress on the second syllable: *re • peat*
- But most English words, especially nouns, with two syllables have stress on the first syllable: *piz • za*.

1 Listen and repeat. The stressed syllables are in **bold.**

   pizza   re**peat**

2 Listen to the words. Underline the stressed syllable in each word.

1. pizza	5. people	9. believe
2. repeat	6. complete	10. ready
3. coffee	7. really	11. ice cream
4. cheesecake	8. season	12. evening

3 Listen again. Repeat the words and check your answers.

4 Circle the correct word in parentheses to complete the rule: Verbs with two syllables often have stress on the (first / second) syllable.

D Role-Play

1 Practice in a group of three or four people.
You are in a restaurant. One person is the waiter or waitress.

2 Talk about what you are going to eat. Use the menu on page 5.

3 The waiter or waitress asks questions. One person orders.
The waiter or waitress repeats the order.

   Example: **A** Are you ready to order?
   B Let's see. We'd like two meat pizzas.
   A Would you like bean soup or Greek salad?
   B Two Greek salads, please.

E The Alphabet

1 Listen to the letters of the alphabet.

A B C D E F G H I J K L M N O P Q R S T U V W X Y Z

2 In American English, nine letters of the alphabet have the sound /iy/ in their names. Circle them in the alphabet above.

3 Listen again. Repeat the letters and check your answers to step **2**.

4 Practice with a partner. Spell your full name. Your partner should write your name as you spell it. Make sure your partner writes it correctly.

F Spelling

The sound /iy/ is usually spelled with the letter *e*. Add more examples below.

ee	three, see, feel, cheese, _____
ea	tea, eat, repeat, please, _____
e	me, we, be, equal
e . . . e	(the second *e* is silent) these, complete, evening

Other spellings:

y	(at the end of a word) very, only, ready, _____
ie	believe, piece, movie
ei	receive, either
ey	key, money
i	visa, machine, police, ski, taxi

Unusual spelling: pe<u>o</u>ple

G Common Expressions

Listen and repeat these common expressions with the sound /iy/.

Really?	I can't bel**ie**ve it.
I agr**ee**.	Pl**ea**sed to m**ee**t you.
Could you rep**ea**t that, pl**ea**se?	Can I pl**ea**se sp**ea**k to L**ee**?

UNIT 2

/ɪ/ • sit

Stress in Numbers; Moving Stress

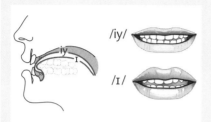

🎧 Practice the sound /iy/.
Open your mouth a little more for /ɪ/.
Do not spread your lips into a smile.
Pull your tongue down a little.
/ɪ/ is a shorter, more relaxed sound than /iy/.
Listen and repeat: /ɪ/.

A Word Pairs

🎧 **1** Listen to these word pairs.

Sound 1: /iy/		Sound 2: /ɪ/	
	sheep	ship	
	seat	sit	
	heel	hill	
	feel	fill	
	sleep	slip	

2 Listen again and repeat.

B Test Yourself

1 Listen to the word pairs. Write *S* if the two words are the same or *D* if the two words are different.

1. _____   2. _____   3. _____   4. _____   5. _____   6. _____

2 Listen to each sentence and circle the word you hear.

1. He isn't going to (leave / live).
2. Try not to (sleep / slip).
3. They want to buy a (sheep / ship).
4. Those (heels / hills) are very high.
5. Did you (feel / fill) the glass?
6. Do you want (a seat / to sit)?

3 Practice step **2** with a partner. Say each sentence, choosing a word from the word pair. Your partner should point to the word you say.

C Vocabulary

Listen and repeat these words with the sound /ɪ/. In words with more than one syllable, the stressed syllable is in **bold**.

is	sick	sit	Mrs. ("**mis**siz")	**lis**ten	fif**teen**
it's	think	miss	**tick**et	**min**utes	be**gin**ning
if	quick	film	be**gins**	**fif**ty	**in**teresting

D Dialog: An interesting film

Two friends have plans to see a film.

1 Work with a partner. Read the dialog. Fill in the blanks with words from task C.

Cindy *(ringing her friend's doorbell)*

Mrs. Kim Hello, Cindy.

Cindy Hi, Mrs. Kim. _____Is_____ William in? Is he coming with me to the film? I picked up a _____ for him.

Mrs. Kim Oh, William's sick.

Cindy Here he is! Hi, William! Are you _____?

William What film is it? Anything _____?

Cindy _____ *King Kong*. And it _____ in fifteen minutes.

William Fifty minutes? Come in and _____ down.

Cindy Not fifty minutes, fifteen!

Mrs. Kim Listen, William, _____ you're sick, I don't think . . .

William Quick! Or we'll miss the _____ of the film!

🎧 **2** Listen to the dialog on page 9 and check your answers.

E Stress in Numbers

Stress can help you hear the difference between numbers ending in -*teen* and -*ty*.

- In -*teen* numbers, the last syllable is usually stressed.
- The *t* in -*teen* has a clear /t/ sound.
- In -*ty* numbers, the first syllable is always stressed.
- The *t* in -*ty* often sounds like a quick /d/ sound.

🎧 Listen and repeat.

13	thir**teen**	30	**thir**ty
14	four**teen**	40	**for**ty
15	fif**teen**	50	**fif**ty
16	six**teen**	60	**six**ty
17	seven**teen**	70	**sev**enty
18	eigh**teen**	80	**eigh**ty
19	nine**teen**	90	**nine**ty

F Moving Stress

In most words, stress does *not* change. However, the stress in -*teen* numbers sometimes changes. It moves to the first syllable when

- counting: **thir**teen, **four**teen, **fif**teen, **six**teen, etc.
- a stressed syllable follows: **fif**teen **min**utes, **four**teen **days**
- the -*teen* number is part of a year: 1915 (**nine**teen **fif**teen).

🎧 Listen and repeat.

A It begins in **fif**teen **min**utes.
B **Fif**ty?
A No, fif**teen**!

G Conversation Practice

Practice this conversation with a partner. Use the -*teen* and -*ty* numbers in task E.

A It begins in _____teen minutes.
B _____ty?
A No, _____teen!

H Bingo Game

1 Play in a group of three to five people.

2 One person will call out the numbers in task E in any order. The other people each choose one of the grids below.

3 When a number is called, cross it out.

4 The first person to cross out all the numbers in a grid calls out "BINGO!" and is the winner.

13	30	80
7	19	50
17	90	8

A

60	4	16
70	7	13
30	18	40

B

14	15	16
70	90	50
40	17	5

C

60	6	15
50	14	18
9	90	80

D

I Spelling

The sound /ɪ/ is usually spelled with the letter *i*. Add more examples below.

i sit, did, will, interesting, minute, _____
       sit – sitting, begin – beginning, win – winner

Other spellings:

y syllable, rhythm, gym
ui building, guilty

Unusual spellings: English, pretty, been, busy, business, women

J Common Expressions

Listen and repeat these common expressions with the sound /ɪ/.

Listen to this.   Do you speak **English**?
Who **is** **it**?   I think **it**'s interesting.
Come **in**.   Where do you live? I live **in** the city.

UNIT 3

/ɛ/ • yes
Falling and Rising Intonation

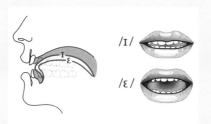

🎧 Practice the sound /ɪ/.
Open your mouth a little more for /ɛ/.
/ɛ/ is a short, relaxed sound.
Listen and repeat: /ɛ/.

A Word Pairs

🎧 **1** Listen to these word pairs.

Sound 1: /ɪ/	Sound 2: /ɛ/
bill	bell
pin	pen
chicks	checks
wrist	rest
spill	spell

2 Listen again and repeat.

B Test Yourself

🎧 **1** Listen and circle the word you hear.

    1. bill / bell   3. wrist / rest   5. spill / spell

    2. pin / pen   4. chicks / checks   6. bitter / better

🎧 **2** Listen to each sentence and circle the word you hear.

    1. I dropped a (pin / pen).

    2. Is that the (bill / bell)?

    3. This coffee tastes (bitter / better).

    4. Her name is (Ginny / Jenny).

    5. Whose (chicks / checks) are these?

    6. He (spilled / spelled) soup.

3 Practice step **2** with a partner. Say each sentence, choosing a word from the word pair. Your partner should point to the word you say.

C Vocabulary

🎧 **1** Listen and repeat these words with the sound /ɛ/. Underline the stressed syllable in each word.

<u>ev</u>er	weather	restaurant	everybody	empty
friendly	yesterday	welcome	especially	excellent
hotel	expensive	everything	any	jealous

2 Listen again. Repeat the words and check your answers.

D Dialog: The best vacation ever!

Jenny just came back from vacation.

🎧 **1** Listen to the dialog. Mark each sentence below *T* for *true* or *F* for *false*. Correct the sentences that are false.

                     Venice

1. ___F___ Jenny went to ~~Mexico~~.

2. _____ She went with her sister.

3. _____ The weather was dry.

4. _____ The hotel was expensive.

5. _____ The restaurants were terrible.

6. _____ She said it was the best vacation ever.

2 Listen again and read the dialog. Check your answers to step **1**.

Jenny Hello, Ben!
Ben Hi, Jenny. Welcome back.
Jenny Thanks!
Ben Where did you spend your vacation?
Jenny I went to Venice with a friend.
Ben Venice? I'm jealous! Tell me everything! When did you get back?
Jenny Yesterday.
Ben How was the weather?
Jenny Wet!
Ben Was it expensive?
Jenny Yes. Very. Especially the hotel.
Ben How were the restaurants?
Jenny They were excellent. But expensive. I spent every cent I had.
Ben So . . . the weather was wet, everything was very expensive, and you don't have any money left. It sounds terrible!
Jenny No. It was the best vacation ever!

E Falling and Rising Intonation

Intonation is the music of language – the way the voice rises (goes up) and falls (goes down) in a phrase or sentence.

- In falling intonation, the voice jumps up on the most important word in the sentence and then falls at the end.
- Statements and *Wh-* questions (questions with *Who? What? Why? When? Where? How?*) usually end with falling intonation.
- In rising intonation, the voice goes up at the end.
- *Yes / No* questions (questions you can answer with *yes* or *no*) usually end with rising intonation.

Listen and repeat.

Wh- question: Where did you spend your va**ca**tion?

Statement: I went to **Ven**ice.

Yes / No question: Was it ex**pen**sive?

Statement: **Yes. Ver**y.

F Conversation Practice

🎧 **1** Listen and repeat these place names.

Mexico	Texas	Yemen	Ecuador
Belgium	Tibet	Kenya	Senegal
Venice	Quebec	Denmark	Central America

2 Practice this conversation with a partner. Use the place names in step **1**.

A Where did you spend your vacation?
B I went to _____.
A Was it expensive?
B Yes. Very. / No. Not very.

G Discussion

Practice in a group of two or three people. Take turns asking and answering questions about your best vacation ever. Use words from task C or other words with the sound /ɛ/.

Example: **A** What was your best vacation ever?
B My trip to Ecuador. It was beautiful! The beaches were empty.
A Were the people friendly?
B Yes. Everybody was very friendly.

H Spelling

The sound /ɛ/ is usually spelled with the letter *e*. Add more examples below.

e   yes, went, spell, expensive, _____
    get – getting

Other spellings:

ea   ready, weather, head, breakfast, _____
a   any, many
ai   said, again

Unusual spellings: s<u>ay</u>s, fr<u>ie</u>nd

I Common Expressions

🎧 Listen and repeat these common expressions with the sound /ɛ/.

Yes.	It's very expensive.
Help!	How do you spell weather?
You're welcome.	Let's get ready.

UNIT 4

/ey/ • day
Stress in Sentences

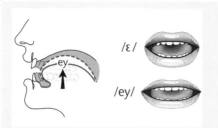

🎧 Practice the sound /ɛ/.
Close your mouth a little for /ey/.
/ey/ is a long sound.
Spread your lips and move your tongue up
     a little as you say it.
Listen and repeat: /ey/.

A Word Pairs

🎧 **1** Listen to these word pairs.

Sound 1: /ɛ/	Sound 2: /ey/
pen	pain
wet	wait
test	taste
pepper	paper
shed	shade

2 Listen again and repeat.

B Test Yourself

1 Listen and circle the word you hear.

1. pen / pain   3. wet / wait   5. test / taste

2. shed / shade   4. pepper / paper   6. sell/ sail

2 Listen to each sentence and circle the word you hear.

1. Can I have some more (pepper / paper)?

2. Put it in the (shed / shade).

3. This (pen / pain) is terrible.

4. Did you see her (letter / later)?

5. I want to (sell / sail) the boat.

6. (Test / Taste) the cake and see if it's done.

3 Practice step **2** with a partner. Say each sentence, choosing a word from the word pair. Your partner should point to the word you say.

C Vocabulary

Listen and repeat these words with the sound /ey/.

today	ages	mistake	vacation
away	train	8:08	changed
May	late	eighth	
April	waiting	station	

D Dialog: At the train station

Jay Davis is waiting for a train.

1 Work with a partner. Read the dialog on pages 17 and 18. Fill in the blanks with words from task C.

Jay Davis Hey! This train is late! I've been waiting here for _____*ages*_____.

Conductor Which train are you _____ for?

Jay Davis The 8:18 to Great Plains.

Conductor The 8:18? I'm afraid you've made a _____, sir.

Jay Davis A mistake? I take this _____ every day!

Conductor The train to Great Plains leaves at _____.

Jay Davis At 8:08? Where does it say that?

Conductor Right here. Train to Great Plains 8:08. They _____ the schedule.

Jay Davis They changed it? I guess they changed it while I was _____ on vacation.

Conductor They changed the schedule at the end of April, sir. _____ is the eighth of May.

Jay Davis Hm! So the train isn't late. *I'm* late.

🎧 **2** Listen to the dialog and check your answers.

E Stress in Sentences

In a sentence, some words are stressed more than others.

- Stressed words sound **louder** and s l o w e r.
- If a stressed word has more than one syllable, only one syllable is stressed.
- The words that are stressed are words that are important for the meaning of the sentence – usually words such as nouns, verbs, adjectives, adverbs, and *wh-* words.
- Structure words such as *a, the, and, but, to, of, it,* and *you* are usually unstressed. They sound quieter and quicker.

Stress in words does not usually change. But sentence stress can change with the speaker's meaning.

🎧 **1** Listen and repeat.

I've been **wait**ing for **ag**es.
I'm a**fraid** you've **made** a mis**take**.
They **changed** the **sched**ule at the **end** of **April**.

🎧 **2** Listen to the sentences. Underline the stressed syllables.

1. To<u>day</u> is the <u>eighth</u> of <u>May</u>.
2. It's my neighbor's birthday.
3. I baked her a cake.
4. But she's going away on vacation.
5. She's going to Spain.
6. Her plane leaves at eight.
7. Can you take her to the airport?
8. I'll give you the cake.

F Conversation Practice

1 Work with a partner. Underline the stressed syllables in each of B's sentences in the conversation.

A Today is the eighth of May.
B The eighth?
A Yes. It's my neighbor's birthday.
B Your neighbor Kate?
A Yes. I baked her a cake.
B A cake?
A But she's going away on vacation.

B She's going away?

A Yes. She's going to Spain.

B To Spain?

A Yes. Her plane leaves at eight.

B At eight today?

A Yes. Can you take her to the airport?

B Me? Maybe.

A I'll give you the cake.

B But you made it for Kate.

A Yes, but she's going away.

B Is it a lemon cake?

A Yes.

B Mm, my favorite! OK, I'll take her!

2 Listen to the conversation and check your answers.

3 Practice the conversation with a partner.

G Spelling

The sound /ey/ is usually spelled with the letter *a*. Add more examples below.

a . . . e	late, name, change, mistake, _____
a	April, later, station, vacation
ay	day, say, away, _____
ai	train, wait, afraid, _____

Other spellings:

eigh	eight, eighteen, weigh, neighbor
ea	great, break, steak
ey	they, hey!, obey

H Common Expressions

Listen and repeat these common expressions with the sound /ey/.

OK.	What's your n**a**me?
W**ai**t!	What's tod**ay**'s d**a**te?
I'm l**a**te.	Have a gr**ea**t d**ay**!

/æ/ • hat

The Most Important Word

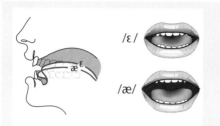

/ɛ/

/æ/

🎧 Practice the sound /ɛ/.
Open your mouth a little more for /æ/.
Listen and repeat: /æ/.

A Word Pairs

🎧 **1** Listen to these word pairs.

Sound 1: /ɛ/		Sound 2: /æ/	
X	x	axe	
	pen	pan	
	men	man	
	left	laughed	
Hi!	said	sad	

2 Listen again and repeat.

B Test Yourself

1 Listen to the word pairs. Write *S* if the two words are the same or *D* if the two words are different.

1. _____ 2. _____ 3. _____ 4. _____ 5. _____ 6. _____

2 Listen to each sentence and circle the word you hear.

1. Where did you put the (pen / pan)?
2. Is that man in the picture (dead / Dad)?
3. He drew an (X / axe) on the board.
4. I talked to the (men / man) in the store.
5. They're (said / sad) to be leaving.
6. She (left / laughed) when I said that.

3 Practice step **2** with a partner. Say each sentence, choosing a word from the word pair. Your partner should point to the word you say.

C Vocabulary

1 Listen and repeat these words with the sound /æ/.

| a hat | a backpack | a black jacket | black pants |
| glasses | a mustache | a plastic bag | a plaid jacket |

2 Work with a partner. Match the pictures with the words in step **1**.

1.   2.  3.   4.

5.   6.   7.   8.

D Dialog: The bank robber

Alice works at a bank. There was a robbery on Saturday. A police detective is asking Alice questions.

1 Listen to the dialog. Check ✓ the items in task C that describe the man who robbed the bank.

2 Listen again and read the dialog. Check your answers to step **1**.

Detective Excuse me, ma'am, do you recognize any of the men in this photograph?
    Alice Yes, that one. That's him! That's the man who robbed the bank!
Detective The man with the black pants?
    Alice Yes. But he had a mustache.
Detective A mustache? This man? Last Saturday?
    Alice Yes. And he was wearing a jacket.
Detective A black jacket?
    Alice No, a plaid jacket. Red plaid.
Detective Can you tell me exactly what happened?
    Alice Well, I was working at the bank on Saturday afternoon. Suddenly, this man ran past me, grabbed a handful of cash, and stuffed it in a bag.
Detective What kind of bag?
    Alice A plastic bag.
Detective And what happened after that?
    Alice He ran back out again. It all happened so fast.
Detective And you're absolutely sure the man in this photograph is the same man?
    Alice Yes. Absolutely. That's him.
Detective Thank you for your help.
    Alice I hope you catch him!

E The Most Important Word

In English, the most important word in the sentence stands out more than other stressed words.

- The stressed syllable of this word is **loud** and s l o w.
- The intonation changes on this word. The voice either jumps up on the stressed syllable and then ⌒↘ falls or jumps down and then rises ↗.
- The most important word is often at the end of a sentence, especially at the beginning of a conversation.
- As a conversation continues, the word that gives new, or added, information becomes the most important word.

1 Listen to these two conversations.

  A He stuffed the cash in a **bag**.   **A** He was wearing a **jack**et.

  B What **kind** of bag?   **B** A **black** jacket?

  A A **plas**tic bag.   **A** **No,** a **plaid** jacket. **Red** plaid.

2 Listen again and repeat.

F Conversation Practice

🎧 **1** Listen to this conversation.

    A That's the person who took my **bag**!

    B Did <u>he</u> have a **hat**?

    A Yes. <u>A</u> **black** <u>hat</u>.

2 Practice the conversation with a partner. Replace the underlined words with the items in the pictures. What is the most important word in each sentence?

a hat (black)

a bag (plastic)

a jacket (plaid)

a hat (red)

a mustache (big)

a jacket (black)

glasses (dark)

a backpack (small)

G Spelling

The sound /æ/ is almost always spelled with the letter *a*. Add more examples below.

    a   hat, man, jacket, glasses, _____
          grab – grabbed, sad – sadder

Unusual spellings: <u>la</u>ugh, pl<u>ai</u>d

H Common Expressions

🎧 Listen and repeat these common expressions with the sound /æ/.

Th**a**nks.	What's the m**a**tter?
Welcome b**a**ck.	I underst**a**nd.
What h**a**ppened?	Do you h**a**ve any plans?

Review
/iy/, /ɪ/, /ɛ/, /ey/, and /æ/

A Test Yourself

1: /iy/	2: /ɪ/	3: /ɛ/	4: /ey/	5: /æ/
lead	lid	led	laid	lad
beat	bit	bet	bait	bat
seal	sill	sell	sail	Sal
dean	din	den	Dane	Dan

🎧 Listen to words from the table. When you hear a word, write the number of its vowel sound.

1. ___(bat) 5___   4. _____   7. _____   10. _____
2. _____   5. _____   8. _____   11. _____
3. _____   6. _____   9. _____   12. _____

B Vocabulary

1 Write each word in the correct column of the table below.

thanks   salad   ready   lettuce
lemon   chicken   back   steak
need   rain   think   sit
great   seat   feel   blanket

1: /iy/	2: /ɪ/	3: /ɛ/	4: /ey/	5: /æ/
				thanks

🎧 **2** Listen. Repeat the words and check your answers.

C Dialog: Dinner on the grass

Anna just came home from work. Ben made dinner.

🎧 **1** Cover the dialog and listen.

Anna Do you need help with dinner?
Ben No thanks. Everything's ready.
Anna Great! Are we having chicken?
Ben No, I made steak.
Ann Any vegetables?
Ben Yes, lettuce and tomato salad. Did you pick up some bread at the bakery?
Anna Yes. And lemon cheesecake.
Ben Lemon cheesecake? That sounds . . . interesting.
Anna I tasted it. It's delicious!
Ben Let's eat in the backyard. OK?
Anna Good idea! It's really pretty this evening.
Ben (*carrying the steak and salad out*) Can you get plates and napkins?
Anna OK. I'll be back in a minute. Should we sit on this seat?
Ben Let's sit on this blanket on the grass.
Anna (*sitting*) Mm. It smells delicious. I can't wait to eat.
        Uh-oh . . . did you feel that? I think it's beginning to rain.
Ben (*standing*) It figures! Can you help me bring everything back in?

2 Read the dialog. Add words from the dialog to the table in task B.

D Syllables and Stress

🎧 Listen. How many syllables does each word have? Write the number of syllables in the space. Then underline the stressed syllable.

1. everything ___3___   4. minute _____   7. tomato _____
2. evening _____   5. beginning _____   8. cheesecake _____
3. salad _____   6. vegetables _____   9. delicious _____

E Puzzle: Which word doesn't belong?

Circle the word in each line that does not have the same vowel sound as the others.

1. seat   steak   idea   cheese
2. pick   pretty   evening   minute
3. jacket   grass   having   bakery
4. any   taste   weather   every
5. eat   feel   jealous   need
6. great   bread   wait   made

/ʌ/ • cup

Strong and Weak Pronunciations

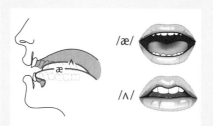

/æ/

/ʌ/

🎧 Practice the sound /æ/.
Close your mouth a little for /ʌ/.
Your tongue should rest in the
middle of your mouth.
/ʌ/ is a short, relaxed sound.
Listen and repeat: /ʌ/.

A Word Pairs

🎧 **1** Listen to these word pairs.

Sound 1: /æ/	Sound 2: /ʌ/
cap	cup
bag	bug
cat	cut
rag	rug
ankle	uncle

2 Listen again and repeat.

B Test Yourself

1 Listen to the word pairs. Write *S* if the two words are the same or *D* if the two words are different.

1. _____   2. _____   3. _____   4. _____   5. _____   6. _____

2 Listen to each sentence and circle the word you hear.

1. Don't sit on the (bag / bug)!
2. This (cap / cup) is too small.
3. I threw away the old (rag / rug).
4. What happened to your (ankle / uncle)?
5. They (ran / run) quickly.
6. How did he get that (cat / cut)?

3 Practice step **2** with a partner. Say each sentence, choosing a word from the word pair. Your partner should point to the word you say.

C Vocabulary

1 One word in each column does *not* have the sound /ʌ/. Work with a partner. Circle the words that do not have the sound /ʌ/.

love	doesn't	young	company
much	don't	enough	cousin
lunch	nothing	talking	once
(happy)	month	brother	your
honey	wonderful	other	understand

2 Listen. Repeat the words and check your answers.

D Dialog: Who does she love?

Russell thinks his girlfriend doesn't love him.

1 Work with a partner. Read the dialog on pages 27 and 28. Fill in the blanks with words from task C. They are all words like *love* that are spelled with the letter *o* but pronounced with the sound /ʌ/.

Jasmine Why are you so unhappy?

Russell (*says nothing*)

Jasmine Honey, why are you so sad?

Russell You don't love me, Jasmine.

Jasmine But Russell, I don't understand. I _____love_____ you very much!

Russell No, you don't. You're in love with my cousin.

Jasmine Justin?

Russell No, my _____ cousin.

Jasmine Duncan?

Russell Don't be funny. He's much too young. I'm talking about his _____.

Jasmine You mean Hunter? That's nuts!

Russell And Hunter loves you, too.

Jasmine No, he _____.

Russell Yes, he does.

Jasmine Russell, just once last _____ I had lunch with Hunter. There's _____ for you to be jealous about.

Russell You think he's fun to be with, and I'm just . . . dull.

Jasmine But honey, I like your _____ much better than Hunter's. I think you're _____.

Russell You do?

🎧 **2** Listen to the dialog and check your answers.

E ▪ Strong and Weak Pronunciations

Many short structure words like the verb *be* (*is, was, were,* etc.), the auxiliary *do* (*do, does,* etc.), and pronouns (*you, he, she,* etc.) have two pronunciations: a strong pronunciation and a weak pronunciation.

- The strong pronunciation is used at the end of a sentence or when the word gets special emphasis. The strong pronunciation has a long, clear vowel sound.
- Otherwise, the weak pronunciation is usually used.
- The weak pronunciation is quieter and quicker. The vowel sound is very short.
- Negative words like *wasn't* and *don't* always have a strong pronunciation.

🎧 Listen and repeat the weak and strong pronunciations.

A Was he jealous?
B Yes, he was.

A Does she love Russell?
B Yes, she does.

A Do they love each other?
B Yes, they do.

He wasn't happy.
It doesn't matter.
I don't understand.

F Scrambled Conversations

🎧 **1** Listen to the questions on the left. Fill in the missing words.

A	B
_____Does he_____ have any brothers?	No, he wasn't.
_____ come here often?	No, she wasn't.
_____ have enough money?	Yes, he does. A younger brother.
_____ late for lunch?	No, I don't. Just once a month.
_____ understand Russian?	Yes, they do. They have two sons.
_____ in love with his cousin?	No, she doesn't, but her husband does.
_____ have any children?	I think I do. How much is it?

2 Practice with a partner. Ask and answer the questions above. Student A asks a question on the left. Student B responds by choosing an answer from the right.

Example: **A** Does he have any brothers?
             B Yes, he does. A younger brother.

🎧 **3** Listen and check your answers.

G Spelling

The sound /ʌ/ is usually spelled with the letter *u* or *o*. Add more examples below.

   u   sun, much, just, funny, _____
         sun – sunny, run – running
   o   love, money, mother, once, done, _____

Other spellings:

   ou country, young, cousin, enough, trouble
   a   was, wasn't, what

Unusual spellings: bl<u>oo</u>d, fl<u>oo</u>d, d<u>oe</u>s, d<u>oe</u>sn't

H Common Expressions

🎧 Listen and repeat these common expressions with the sound /ʌ/.

What **co**untry are you fr**o**m?
What's **u**p? N**o**thing m**u**ch.
That was f**u**n!

Do you have en**ou**gh m**o**ney?
Would you like an**o**ther **o**ne?
I l**o**ve it!

/ə/ • a banana

/ə/ in Unstressed Syllables and Words; *can* and *can't*

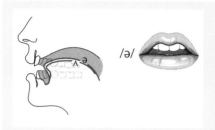

🎧 Practice the sound /ʌ/.
Make it very short for /ə/.
The sound /ə/ is always short and weak.
Listen and repeat: /ə/.

A Vocabulary

🎧 **1** The sound /ə/ is used in many unstressed syllables and words. In the words below, the spelling has been changed to show you when to use the sound /ə/. Stressed syllables are in bold. Listen and repeat.

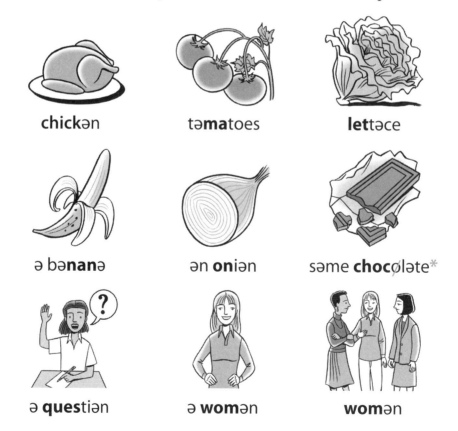

chickən tə**ma**toes **let**təce

ə bə**nan**ə ən **on**iən səme **choc**øləte*

ə **ques**tiən ə **wom**ən **wom**ən

* A slash through a letter means it is not pronounced.

B /ə/ in Unstressed Syllables and Words

/ə/ is the most common vowel sound in English.

- It is used in many unstressed syllables in words.
- It is also used in the weak pronunciation of many short structure words, such as *a, an, of,* and *and.* These words almost always have a weak pronunciation with the sound /ə/.

🎧 **1** Listen and repeat.

ə cup əf coffee

ə can əf sodə

ə pound əf oniəns

bacən ənd eggs

chips ənd salsə

chocəlate ənd vənillə

2 Practice with a partner. Complete the phrases.

ə _____ əf _____

ə _____ əf _____

ə _____ əf _____

_____ ənd _____

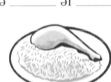

_____ ənd _____

_____ ənd _____

🎧 **3** Listen. Repeat the phrases and check your answers.

C can and can't

> - *Can* is usually unstressed and has a weak pronunciation when another word follows it in a sentence. The vowel sound is reduced to /ə/.
> - *Can* has a strong pronunciation when it is at the end of a sentence. It has the clear vowel sound /æ/.
> - *Can't* always has a strong pronunciation. It has the clear vowel sound /æ/.
>
> The difference in vowel sounds can help you hear the difference between *can* and *can't*.

1 Listen and repeat.

She cən ride ə bike.

She cən play thə guətar.

She cən sail ə boat.

She can't drive ə car.

She can't play thə piano.

She can't swim.

2 Listen and repeat.

A Cən she ride ə bike?   **B** Yes, she can.

A Cən she drive ə car?   **B** No, she can't.

D Test Yourself

1 Listen to each sentence and circle the word you hear.

1. He (can / can't) play the piano.
2. I (can / can't) stand on my head.
3. She (can / can't) ride a horse.
4. She (can / can't) speak Japanese, but her children (can / can't).
5. You (can / can't) park your car here.
6. I (can / can't) meet you at three o'clock.

2 Practice step **1** with a partner. Say each sentence, choosing a word from the word pair. Your partner should point to the word you say.

E Discussion

1 Practice in a group of three to five people. List things you can and can't do.

Example: I can ride a bike.
I can't ride a horse.

Use the examples in task C, the ideas below, or your own ideas.

ride a bike	ride a horse
drive a car	drive a truck
play the piano	play the guitar
swim	sail a boat
do a handstand	do karate
bake a cake	speak three languages

2 Tell the class what all of you, some of you, and none of you can do.

Example: **A** All of us can swim.
B Two of us can play the piano.
C One of us can ride a horse.
A None of us can do a handstand.

F Spelling

The sound /ə/ can be spelled with any vowel letter. Add more examples below.

a about, again, banana, woman, _____

e problem, open, excellent, women, _____

i possible, animal, notice, guitar

o today, computer, question, welcome, _____

u suggest, success, careful, lettuce

Other spelling:

ou famous, delicious, dangerous

G Common Expressions

Listen and repeat these common expressions with the sound /ə/.

What's the problem?	That's an excellent question.
Go away!	I'm from Canada.
Can you say that again?	the United States of America

UNIT 9 /ər/ • letter

/ər/ in Unstressed Syllables and Words;
Intonation in Choice Questions with *or*

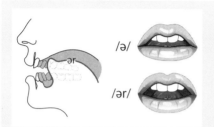

🎧 Practice the short sound /ə/.
Curl the tip of your tongue up and back to say /ər/.
The sound /ər/ is pronounced as one short sound.
Listen and repeat: /ər/.

A Vocabulary

🎧 **1** The sound /ər/ is used in many unstressed syllables spelled with a vowel + *r*. In the words below, the spelling has been changed to show you when to use the sound /ər/. Listen and repeat.

waitər	**law**yər	**act**ər	**farm**ər
doctər	**teach**ər	**paint**ər	re**port**ər

2 Work with a partner. What is each person's job? Match the pictures with the words in step **1**.

Example: 1. She's a painter.

1.   2.   3.   4.

5.   6.   7.   8.

B /ər/ in Unstressed Syllables and Words

- The sound /ər/ is used in many unstressed syllables spelled with a vowel + *r*.
- It is also used in the weak pronunciation of many short structure words spelled with a vowel + *r*, such as *are*, *for*, and *or*.
- The word *or* is usually unstressed and pronounced as the sound /ər/. It sounds the same as the unstressed ending *-er* in *teacher*.

∩ **1** Listen and repeat.

soup ər salad   large ər small   married ər single

2 Practice with a partner. Complete the phrases.

coffee ər _____   one ər _____   right ər _____

summər ər _____   Satərday ər _____   chocolate ər _____

∩ **3** Listen. Repeat the phrases and check your answers.

C Intonation in Choice Questions with *or*

Questions with *or* that ask the listener to make a choice have rising intonation on the first choice and falling intonation on the last choice.

1 Listen and repeat these two conversations.

A Would you like **cof**fee or **tea**?

B **Tea**, please.

A Are you **mar**ried or **sin**gle?

B **Mar**ried.

2 Practice with a partner. Ask a choice question with *or* about each pair of items in task B. Begin your question with phrases like these:

Would you like . . . ?   Is it . . . ?

Do you want . . . ?   Are you . . . ?

D Dialog: Asking a favor

Spencer asks his roommate to get some things at the supermarket.

1 Weak pronunciations usually have the sound /ə/ or /ər/. In the words on the right, the spelling has been changed to show you when to use the sound /ə/ or /ər/. Listen and repeat these phrases.

to the doctor	tə thə doctər
for me	fər me
at the supermarket	ət thə supərmarkət
on your way	on yər way
do you want	də yə want
Where are you going?	Where ərə yə going?

Shopping List

bread

tuna fish

peanut butter

yogurt

2 Listen to the dialog. Notice the /ə/ and /ər/ sounds.

Tyler	See you later.
Spencer	Where are you going?
Tyler	To the doctor.
Spencer	Can you get something for me at the supermarket on your way home?
Tyler	OK. What do you want me to get?
Spencer	I need some bread.
Tyler	Do you want white bread or whole wheat?
Spencer	Whole wheat. And can you get a couple of cans of tuna fish?
Tyler	Do you want tuna packed in oil or water?
Spencer	Water. Oh, and a jar of peanut butter and a container of vanilla yogurt.
Tyler	Hey, that's a lot of stuff!
Spencer	And one more thing – a pint of ice cream.
Tyler	What flavor do you want?
Spencer	What flavor do you like?
Tyler	Me?
Spencer	Yes, the ice cream is for you. To thank you for stopping at the supermarket.

3 Listen to the dialog again. Add more phrases that use the sound /ə/ or /ər/ to the list in step **1**.

4 Practice the dialog with a partner.

E Spelling

The unstressed sound /ər/ is usually spelled *er* or *or*. Add more examples below.

er   answer, teacher, mother, after, _____

or   doctor, visitor, calculator, memory, _____

Other spellings:

ar   dollar, popular, sugar, liar

ur(e) picture, measure, future, Saturday

F Common Expressions

Listen and repeat these common expressions with the sound /ər/.

See you lat**er**.	Do you know the answ**er**?
Don't f**or**get.	Are you married **or** single?
What's f**or** dinn**er**?	Do you have any broth**ers or** sist**ers**?

UNIT 10

/ɑ/ • hot

Phrase Groups

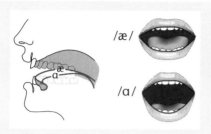

🎧 Practice the sound /æ/.
Open your mouth wide for the sound /ɑ/.
Your tongue should rest in the bottom of
   your mouth.
Listen and repeat: /ɑ/.

A Word Pairs 1

🎧 **1** Listen to these word pairs.

Sound 1: /æ/	Sound 2: /ɑ/
hat	hot
cat	cot
cap	cop
sack	sock
ran	Ron

2 Listen again and repeat.

B Word Pairs 2

🎧 **1** Listen to these word pairs.

Sound 1: /ʌ/	**Sound 2: /ɑ/**
hut	hot
cut	cot
cup	cop
suck	sock

2 Listen again and repeat.

C Test Yourself

🎧 **1** Listen and circle the word you hear.

1. cat / cut / cot   3. cap / cup / cop   5. hat / hut / hot

2. ran / run / Ron   4. sack / suck / sock   6. Dan / done / Don

🎧 **2** Listen to each sentence and circle the word you hear.

1. Don't sit on the (cat / cot)!

2. He keeps his money in a (sack / sock).

3. That (color / collar) looks good on you.

4. There's a (duck / dock) on the lake.

5. Did you see that (cap / cup / cop)?

6. Is that (Dan / done / Don)?

3 Practice step **2** with a partner. Say each sentence, choosing a word from the word pair. Your partner should point to the word you say.

D Vocabulary

1 Listen and repeat these words with the sound /ɑ/.

a doll   a watch   a novel

a teapot   a laptop   a box of chocolates

2 Listen and repeat. Curl the tip of your tongue up to make the sound /r/ in these words.

a scarf   a guitar   a deck of cards

3 Work with a partner. Match the pictures with the words in steps **1** and **2**.

1.   2.   3.   4.   5.

6.   7.   8.   9.

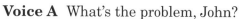

E Dialog: A TV commercial

In this TV commercial, John is shopping for holiday presents.

1 Cover the dialog and listen. Check ✓ the items in task D that you hear in the dialog.

2 Listen again and read the dialog. Check your answers to step **1**.

Voice A What's the problem, John?

John It's this holiday shopping – I'm ready to drop!

Voice B Just stop!

Voice A Don't shop till you drop.

Voice B Park your car in your garage, turn on the nonstop shopping channel, and start shopping the modern way!

Voice A Whether you're looking for a watch for your father,

Voice B a laptop for your mother,

Voice A a guitar for your brother,

Voice B or a box of chocolates for your sweetheart,

Voice A we've got what you want! The best products at bargain prices!

Voice B We'll show you what's hot and what's not.

Voice A Do you have a lot of gifts to buy? It's not a hard job with the shopping channel.

Voice B Or shop online at our popular Web site. Just log on to *www.nonstopshopping.com*.

F Phrase Groups

To make long sentences easier to say and understand, break them up into phrase groups.

- Words in a phrase group are linked together, with no pauses between the words.
- At least one word in a phrase group is stressed.

🎧 Listen and repeat.

John went **shop**ping /and he **spent** / a **lot** of **mon**ey. /
He got a **watch** / for his **fa**ther / a **lap**top / for his **moth**er / and a **nov**el / for his **son**. /

G Game: "John went shopping"

Play this game in groups of four or five people. Choose a phrase from box 1 and a phrase from box 2 below. Each person adds something new.

Example: **A** John went shopping and he spent a lot of money. He got a teapot for his aunt.
B John went shopping and he spent a lot of money. He got a teapot for his aunt and some socks for his cousin.

1			2	
a **clock**	a **tea**pot	a **deck** of **cards**	for his **father**	for his **son**
a **lap**top	a **nov**el	a **box** of **pas**ta	for his **mother**	for his **daugh**ter
a **watch**	a **wal**let	a **box** of **choc**olates	for his **brother**	for his **cous**in
a gui**tar**	a **scarf**	some **socks**	for his **aunt**	for his **grand**mother
a **car**	a **doll**	**tick**ets to a **rock** concert	for his **un**cle	for his **grand**father

H Spelling

The sound /ɑ/ is usually spelled with the letter *o* or *a*. Add more examples below.

o stop, job, clock, popular, chocolate*, _____
shop – shopping, stop – stopped, hot – hotter

a father, want*, watch*, wallet*
(before *r*) car, star, hard, large, _____

*Some people say these words with the sound /ɔ/, not /ɑ/.

I Common Expressions

🎧 Listen and repeat these common expressions with the sound /ɑ/.

Stop!	What do you w**a**nt?
No pr**o**blem!	Are you coming? Pr**o**bably n**o**t.
I g**o**t a j**o**b.	Park the c**a**r.

UNIT 11

/ɔ/ • ball

Using Stress and Intonation to Show a Contrast

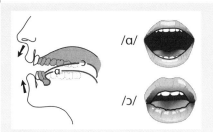

🎧 Practice the sound /ɑ/.
Pull your tongue back a little for /ɔ/.
Push your lips forward a little
   and make them round.
Listen and repeat: /ɔ/. *

A Word Pairs 1

🎧 **1** Listen to these word pairs.

	Sound 1: /ʌ/	Sound 2: /ɔ/	
	cut	caught	
	dug	dog	
	bus	boss	
	done	dawn	
	color	caller	

2 Listen again and repeat.

* In words without *r* after the vowel, many people in the U.S. and Canada use the sound /ɑ/ instead of /ɔ/.

B Word Pairs 2

🎧 **1** Listen to these word pairs.

Sound 1: /ɑr/	**Sound 2: /ɔr/**
far	four
star	store
card	cord
part	port

2 Listen again and repeat. Curl the tip of your tongue up to make the sound /r/ in these words.

C Test Yourself

🎧 **1** Listen and circle the word you hear.

1. cut / caught   3. color / caller   5. card / cord
2. bus / boss   4. far / four   6. star / store

🎧 **2** Listen to each sentence and circle the word you hear.

1. I'm waiting for the (bus / boss).
2. He (cut / caught) the paper.
3. Is it (far / four)?
4. This needs a new (card / cord).
5. Did you get the name of the (color / caller)?
6. Isn't it (done / dawn) yet?

3 Practice step **2** with a partner. Say each sentence, choosing a word from the word pair. Your partner should point to the word you say.

D Vocabulary

🎧 Listen and repeat these words with the sound /ɔ/.

lost	falling	airport	sports	awful	fault
small	walking	reporter	toward	thought	always

American Football

a quarterback

SCORE

BOSTON HAWKS	4
NEW YORK HORSES	44

the scoreboard

the ball

E Dialog: Sports report on Channel 4

Laura is a sports reporter. She is talking to a football player after a game.

🎧 **1** Read the dialog as you listen to the sports report. If you hear a word that is different from the word in your book, correct the word. Use the words in task D. There are 13 words to correct. The first one has been done for you.

Hawks

Announcer This morning the ~~Horses~~ returned from their game in Boston.

Laura Morgan, our sports reporter, was at the store to meet them.

Laura Good morning. I'm Laura Morgan. All the baseball players are running

toward me. Here's George Tall, the halfback. Good morning, George.

George Good morning. Are you a reporter?

Laura Yes, I'm from Channel 1. Can you tell our audience what you thought about

the game in Boston?

George It was fun! We won. The score was 4 to 40.

Laura Really? I thought the score was 4 to 34.

George No, 4 to 40. But it wasn't my fault.

Laura Whose fault was it?

George The quarterback's.

Laura The quarterback's?

George Yes, the quarterback's. He was always talking or dropping the ball.

2 Listen again and check your answers.

F Using Stress and Intonation to Show a Contrast

When speaking, people make the information or word that is *new* or *different* stand out.

- The stressed syllable of this word sounds extra **loud** and s l o w.
- The intonation changes on this word. In a sentence with falling intonation, the voice jumps up on the stressed syllable of the word and then falls.

1 Listen. In these three conversations, Speaker B makes the information that is *different* stand out.

A George played baseball in **Bos**ton.

B I thought George played **foot**ball in Boston.

A George played football in New **York**.

B I thought George played football in **Bos**ton.

A Paul played football in **Bos**ton.

B I thought **George** played football in Boston.

2 Listen again and repeat.

G Conversation Practice

1 Work with a partner. Circle the word that should stand out in Speaker B's sentences.

1. **A** The reporter's name was **George**.
   B I thought the (football) player's name was George.

2. **A** New York lost the **game**.
   B I thought Boston lost the game.

3. **A** The score was 8 to **4**4.

   B I thought the score was 4 to 44.

4. **A** George played football in the **eve**ning.

   B I thought he played football in the morning.

5. **A** George talked to Corey at the **air**port.

   B I thought he talked to Laura at the airport.

6. **A** It wasn't George's **fault**.

   B I thought it was George's fault.

2 Practice the conversations in step **1**.

H Spelling

The sound /ɔ/ is usually spelled with the letters *o, au, aw,* or *a*. Add more examples below.

    o   long, across, lost, dog, _____

               before the letter *r*: sports, morning, more, before, _____

    au   fault, because, August, caught, _____

    aw   saw, awful, draw, dawn

    a   before the letter *l*: ball, also, walk*, talk*, _____

               before the letter *r*: warm, war, quarter

Other spellings:

    ough thought, bought, fought

    ou   before the letter *r*: four, your, of course

Unusual spellings: t<u>ow</u>ard, br<u>oa</u>d, d<u>oo</u>r, fl<u>oo</u>r

* The letter *l* in these words is silent.

I Common Expressions

🎧 Listen and repeat these common expressions with the sound /ɔ/.

What's wr**o**ng?	Good m**or**ning.
Who's c**a**lling?	Of c**ou**rse!
You have the wr**o**ng number.	Have some m**o**re c**o**ffee.

/ow/ • go
Linking Vowel Sounds

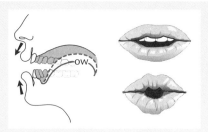

🎧 Practice the sound /ɔ/.
Close your mouth a little for /ow/.
/ow/ is a long sound.
As you say it, push your lips forward into a circle.
Listen and repeat: /ow/.

A Word Pairs

🎧 **1** Listen to these word pairs.

Sound 1: /ɔ/*	Sound 2: /ow/
saw	sew
caught	coat
hall	hole
ball	bowl
walk	woke

2 Listen again and repeat.

* Many people in the U.S. and Canada use the sound /a/ instead of /ɔ/ in these words.

B Test Yourself

🎧 **1** Listen to the word pairs. Write *S* if the two words are the same or *D* if the two words are different.

1. _____ 2. _____ 3. _____ 4. _____ 5. _____ 6. _____

🎧 **2** Listen to each sentence and circle the word you hear.

1. I fell in the (hall / hole).
2. Could you (saw / sew) this for me?
3. Don't drop the (ball / bowl)!
4. I (walk / woke) early in the morning.
5. Were you (called / cold)?
6. Do you know anything about the (cost / coast)?

3 Practice step **2** with a partner. Say each sentence, choosing a word from the word pair. Your partner should point to the word you say.

C Vocabulary

1 One word in each column does *not* have the sound /ow/. Work with a partner. Circle the words that do not have the sound /ow/.

Oh, no!	over	only	closed
snow	open	come	throw
hello	problem	woke	now
ago	going	joking	don't
stop	window	coat	October

🎧 **2** Listen. Repeat the words and check your answers.

D Dialog: Snow

Joan woke up a few minutes ago, but Joe is still sleeping.

🎧 **1** Cover the dialog on the next page and listen. Mark each sentence below *T* for *true* or *F* for *false*. Correct the sentences that are false.

                        snowing
1. __F__ It's ~~raining~~.

2. _____ Joe's eyes are open.

3. _____ It's November.

4. _____ Joan is joking.

5. _____ Joe wants to go back to sleep.

6. _____ Joan is going to put on her robe.

7. _____ Joan is going to go outside.

OCTOBER

S	M	T	W	T	F	S
		1	2	3	4	5	6
7	8	9	10	11	12	13
14	15	16	17	18	19	20
21	22	23	24	25	26	27
28	29	30	31			

Joan Joe! Joe! JOE! Hello!?

Joe (*groans*) Oh, no. What's the problem?

Joan Look out the window.

Joe No. My eyes are closed, and I'm going back to sleep.

Joan Don't go to sleep now, Joe. Come look at the snow.

Joe Snow? It's only October. I know there's no snow. Leave me alone.

Joan Come over to the window.

Joe Stop joking, Joan. There's no snow.

Joan OK, I'll show you. I'm going to put on my coat and go out and make a snowball and throw it at you! Then you'll open your eyes!

2 Listen again and check your answers to step **1**.

E Linking Vowel Sounds

When one word ends with a vowel sound and the next word begins with a vowel sound, link the two vowels smoothly without a break.

- When the sound /ow/ comes before another vowel sound, use the /w/ sound to link the two vowels together.

1 Listen and repeat.

/w/
go out

/w/
throw it

2 Read the sentences. Draw a linking line to show where the sound /ow/ can be linked to a following vowel.

1. There was no answer.
2. No I don't.
3. Do you know everyone?
4. Sure, go ahead.
5. Is the window open?

6. It's so annoying.
7. We can't go in.
8. Is there snow on the ground?
9. Joe isn't home.
10. No, are you cold?

3 Listen. Repeat the sentences and check your answers.

F Scrambled Conversations

1 Practice with a partner. Student A says a sentence on the left. Student B responds with a sentence from the right.

A	B
Do you know everyone here?	Sure, go ahead.
Hello. Can I speak to Joe?	Yes, but there was no answer.
Is it OK if I take one?	No, I don't.
Is the window open?	No, it's only snowing a little.
Did you call Joan?	No, are you cold?
Is there snow on the ground?	I know. It's so annoying.
We can't go in yet.	Sorry, Joe isn't home now.

2 Listen and check your answers.

G Spelling

The sound /ow/ is usually spelled with the letter *o*. Add more examples below.

o   go, open, joking, told, don't, _____

o . . . e home, those, joke, phone, _____

oa   boat, coat, road, coast

ow   know, show, window, _____

Other spelling:

oe   toe, Joe

Unusual spellings: shoulder, though, sew, oh!

H Common Expressions

Listen and repeat these common expressions with the sound /ow/.

No.	I'm **o**nly j**o**king.
I d**o**n't kn**ow**.	How's it g**o**ing? **O**K.
I h**o**pe s**o**.	Could you **o**pen the wind**ow**?

UNIT 13

/uw/ • too

Stress and Pronouns

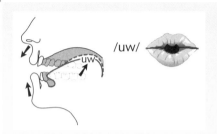

🎧 Push your lips forward into a circle.
Pull your tongue up and back.
/uw/ is a long sound.
Push your lips into a tighter circle as you say it.
Listen and repeat: /uw/.

A Vocabulary

🎧 **1** Listen and repeat these words with the sound /uw/.

too	blue shoes	Tuesday	Happy New Year
soon	student	introduce	What's new?
food	movie	roommate	What do you do?

🎧 **2** These words have a /y/ sound before the /uw/: /yuw/. Listen and repeat.

computer	music	usual	excuse me

B Dialog: Happy New Year!

Friends are talking at a New Year's Eve party.

1 Work with a partner. Read the short conversations on pages 51 and 52. Fill in each blank with the correct sentence from the list below.

1. No, are you?
2. Happy New Year!
3. What do you do?
4. Is she a student, too?

5. Nice to meet you, too!
6. Yes. Do you like it?
7. What's new?
8. Nice to meet you, Lou.

9. Thank you.
10. Excuse me.

Happy New Year!

Happy New Year to you, too!

This is Lou. He's from Peru.

Just the usual. What's new with you?

Do you like this music?

🎧 **2** Listen to the conversations and check your answers.

C Stress and Pronouns

- Pronouns like *I, you, we,* and *them* are usually unstressed and have a weak pronunciation.
- When *you* is not at the end of a sentence, the vowel sound is often reduced to /ə/.
- Pronouns are stressed when the speaker wants to emphasize them or make a contrast.

🎧 **1** Listen. Notice the weak pronunciation of *you* in A's question and the strong pronunciation of *you* in B's question.

        /də yə/

A **What** do you **do**?

                        /də yuw/

B I **work** with com**put**ers. **What** do **you** do?

2 Listen again and repeat.

D Conversation Practice

1 Work with a partner. The first line in each conversation is missing. Look at B's response. Then fill in A's missing line with your own ideas.

1. **A** _Happy New Year!_
   B Happy New Year to you, too!

2. **A** _____
   B Thank you. It's new.

5. **A** _____
   B Nice to meet you.

6. **A** _____
   B Yes. Do you?

3. **A** _____
   B I'm a student. What about you?

4. **A** _____
   B Nice to meet you, too.

7. **A** _____
   B Really? Me, too.

8. **A** _____
   B No. Are you?

2 Practice the conversations with your partner. Where should the pronoun *you* be stressed?

E Spelling

The sound /uw/ is usually spelled with the letters *oo* or *u*. Add more examples below.

oo   too, soon, school, choose, _____

u   student, truth, music*, u̲sually*,_____

u . . . e introduce, true, use*, confused*,_____

Other spellings:

o   do, who, movie, two

o . . . e move, whose, lose, shoe

ou   you, group, soup

ew   new, knew, grew, few*

Unusual spellings: thr**ough**, j**ui**ce, fr**ui**t, s**ui**t, b**eau**tiful*

*These words have a /y/ sound before the /uw/ : /yuw/.

F Common Expressions

🎧 Listen and repeat these common expressions with the sound /uw/.

Exc**u**se me.   Wh**o** is it?*
What's n**ew**?   See you s**oo**n.
What do you d**o**?   Let me introd**u**ce **you**.

*When the sound /uw/ comes before another vowel sound, use the /w/ sound in /uw/ to link the two vowels together.

/ʊ/ • book

Negative Contractions

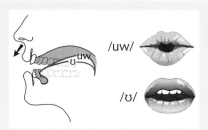

🎧 Practice the sound /uw/.
Open your mouth a little more for /ʊ/.
Your lips should be less round.
Do not push them into a tight circle.
/ʊ/ is a shorter, more relaxed sound than /uw/.
Listen and repeat: /ʊ/.

A Word Pairs

🎧 **1** Listen to these word pairs.

Sound 1: /uw/	**Sound 2:** /ʊ/
Luke	look
pool	pull
fool	full
suit	soot
stewed	stood

2 Listen again and repeat.

B Test Yourself

🎧 **1** Listen to the word pairs. Write *S* if the two words are the same or *D* if the two words are different.

1. _____   2. _____   3. _____   4. _____   5. _____   6. _____

🎧 **2** Listen to each sentence and circle the word you hear.

1. The sign on the door says ("Pool" / "Pull").
2. (Luke / Look), I want you to come here.
3. Where did that black (suit / soot) come from?
4. I think he's (a fool / full).
5. I (stewed / stood) the vegetables in the pot.
6. She stepped on my (food / foot).

3 Practice step **2** with a partner. Say each sentence, choosing a word from the word pair. Your partner should point to the word you say.

C Vocabulary

1 One word in each column does *not* have the sound /ʊ/. Work with a partner. Circle the words that do not have the sound /ʊ/.

look	sugar	food	wouldn't
put	shouldn't	good	cookies
enough	cookbook	full	under
could	use	took	cushion

🎧 **2** Listen. Repeat the words and check your answers.

D Dialog: Looking for a book

Julia can't find her cookbook. She asks Luke to help her look for it.

🎧 **1** Listen to the dialog. Fill in the blanks with: *should, shouldn't, could, couldn't, would,* or *wouldn't.*

Julia Luke, _____could_____ you help me look for my book? I'm not sure where I put it.

Luke Which book?

Julia My new cookbook – *Good Cooking.*

Luke _____ I look in the bookcase?

Julia No, the bookcase is full. It _____ be there.

Luke Maybe you _____ look in the living room.

Julia I looked everywhere, even under the cushions.

Luke _____ you use another cookbook?

Julia No, the cookbook I'm looking for is a sugar-free, fat-free –

Luke (*interrupting*) – food-free cookbook?

Julia Very funny. You eat too much junk food. It isn't good for you.

Luke But it tastes good!

Julia Well, you _____ eat so much sugar. Hmm . . . I think you took that book and put it somewhere so I _____ use it.

Luke I didn't put it anywhere! (*pause*) I think you _____ look under that box of cookies.

Julia (*picking up the cookies*) Oops.

2 Listen again and check your answers.

E Negative Contractions

- In English, people usually use contractions (like *it's* or *couldn't*) rather than long forms (like *it is* or *could not*) when they speak.
- Contractions with *not* always have a strong pronunciation, even if the main word in the contraction usually has a weak pronunciation.

🎧 **1** Listen to the difference between these pairs of sentences.

I **could**n't **use** it.	I could **use** it.
It **would**n't **fit** there.	It would **fit** there.
You **should**n't **eat** the **cook**ies.	You should **eat** the **cook**ies.

🎧 **2** Listen to each sentence and circle the word you hear.

1. I (could / couldn't) get a job as a cook.
2. I (would / wouldn't) wear a suit to school.
3. You (could / couldn't) learn to cook from a book.
4. You (should / shouldn't) eat a lot of fruit.
5. You (should / shouldn't) drink a lot of juice.
6. You (could / couldn't) make good cookies without sugar.

3 Listen again. Repeat the sentences and check your answers.

F Conversation Practice

1 Practice with a partner. Say the sentences in step **2** of task E to your partner. Choose the word that you think makes the sentence true.

2 Practice the sentences in a group of three or four people. Complete the sentences with your own ideas.

Example: I wouldn't wear blue shoes.

I wouldn't wear _____.

You should eat _____.

You shouldn't eat _____.

You couldn't learn _____ from a book.

G Rhythm Chant

🎧 **1** The pattern of stressed and unstressed syllables helps give English its rhythm. Listen.

You **should**n't eat **too** many **cook**ies.
You **should**n't eat **too** much **fruit**.
You **should**n't eat **too** much **sug**ar.
You **should**n't drink **too** much **j**uice.
It's **not good** for you.
It's **not good** for me? **Says who**?
This book. Take a **look**.

Which words in bold have the sound /ʊ/? _____

2 Practice the chant. Put stress only on the words in bold.

H Spelling

The sound /ʊ/ is usually spelled with the letters *oo* or *u*. Add more examples below.

oo*   good, look, book, foot, _____

u   pull, push, sugar, put, _____

Unusual spellings: should, could, would, woman

*A few words spelled with *oo* can be pronounced either with the sound /ʊ/ or /uw/: *room, roof, root*.

I Common Expressions

🎧 Listen and repeat these common expressions with the sound /ʊ/.

Look!   I **could**n't do it.
Who's that w**o**man?   **Put** some **sug**ar in it.
That's a **good** b**oo**k.   Those **cook**ies **look good**.

UNIT 15 Review

/ʌ/, /ɑ/, /ɔ/, /ow/, /uw/, /ʊ/, and /ə/

A Test Yourself

1: /ʌ/	2: /ɑ/	3: /ɔ/*	4: /ow/*	5: /uw/	6: /ʊ/
uh . . .	ah!	aw!	oh!	ooh!	
luck	lock	law	low	Luke	look
done	Don	dawn	don't	dune	
	Polly	Paul	pole	pool	pull
	folly	fall	foal	fool	full

🎧 Listen to words from the table. When you hear a word, write the number of its vowel sound.

1. ___(ooh!) 5___   4. _____   7. _____   10. _____

2. _____   5. _____   8. _____   11. _____

3. _____   6. _____   9. _____   12. _____

B Vocabulary

1 One word in each phrase below normally has the unstressed sound /ə/. Underline the word that is usually pronounced with the sound /ə/.

opposite <u>the</u> window   push and pull

full of books   too hard to move

we can move   Don't you think?

a few things   What should I do?

🎧 **2** Listen. Repeat the phrases and check your answers.

*Many people in the U.S. and Canada use the sound /ɑ/ instead of /ɔ/ in these words.

C Dialog: Paul's new apartment

Paul's mother is visiting his new apartment.

🎧 **1** Cover the dialog and listen.

Mother So, this is your new apartment.

Paul Yes, my own apartment! Isn't it wonderful?

Mother (*pausing*) It's . . . uh . . . it has a lovely view.

Paul I know the rooms are small, but –

Mother We can move a few things, and the room will look much larger.

Paul But –

Mother You know, the sofa should always be opposite the window.

Paul Oh, the sofa is too hard to move.

Mother Nonsense. I'll push and you pull.

Paul (*pulling*) Ugh!

Mother Now let's move the bookcase to the other wall.

Paul But the bookcase is full of books.

Mother Oh, no problem. We'll just put them on the floor.

Paul Um, OK.

Mother (*moving the books*) That's done. And that photo – it doesn't look good over the blue sofa.

Paul It doesn't? What should I do with it?

Mother Why don't you put it on top of the bookcase?
Ah, that's much better!
(*looking at Paul*) What's wrong? Don't you think it looks good?

Paul Oh, beautiful. But . . . I thought the room looked good before we moved everything!

2 Read the dialog. Add words from the dialog to the table in task A.

D Puzzle: Which word doesn't belong?

Circle the word in each line that does not have the same vowel sound as the others.

1. just	sometimes	(put)	much	wonderful
2. not	opposite	problem	closed	nonsense
3. blue	move	love	do	new
4. nothing	just	doesn't	under	don't
5. book	food	full	push	good
6. own	over	phone	done	those
7. small	wrong	wall	should	thought

UNIT 16

/ay/ • fine

Stress in Compound Nouns

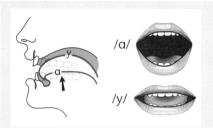

🎧 /ay/ has two sounds: /a/ and /y/.
Practice the sound /a/. Make this sound long.
Add /y/. Make this sound short.
Listen and repeat: /ay/.

A Word Pairs

🎧 **1** Listen to these word pairs.

Sound 1: /æ/		**Sound 2: /ay/**	
	hat	height	
	back	bike	
	van	vine	
	cat	kite	
	pants	pints	

2 Listen again and repeat.

B Test Yourself

1 Listen and circle the word you hear.

1. van / vine   3. pants / pints   5. cat / kite
2. hat / height   4. back / bike   6. sad / side

2 Listen to each sentence and circle the word you hear.

1. Carry it on your (back / bike).
2. Is this your (hat / height)?
3. My (cat / kite) got stuck in a tree.
4. They don't sell (pants / pints).
5. There's a (van / vine) next to the house.
6. They (had / hide) the money.

3 Practice step **2** with a partner. Say each sentence, choosing a word from the word pair. Your partner should point to the word you say.

C Vocabulary

1 Listen and repeat the names of these activities.

hiking	climbing	kayaking
bike riding	skydiving	scuba diving
horseback riding	ice skating	hang gliding

2 Work with a partner. Match the pictures with the words in step **1**.

1.   2.   3.   4.   5.

6.   7.   8.   9.

D Dialog: Exercise . . . or ice cream?

Liza and Mike are talking about plans for after work.

1 Listen to the dialog. Then answer the questions.

1. What does Liza invite Mike to do? Check ✓ the activities in task C.
2. What does Mike decide to do?

🎧 **2** Listen again and read the dialog. Check your answers to step **1**.

Liza Hi, Mike. How are you?
Mike Oh, hi, Liza. I'm fine, thanks.
Liza Mike, do you like hiking?
Mike Sometimes. Why?
Liza I'm going hiking later. Would you like to come?
Mike Maybe some other time. I have 19 e-mails to write by five o'clock.
Liza Would you like to go ice skating tonight?
Mike I've never tried ice skating.
Liza Why not try it tonight?
Mike Not tonight, Liza. I'm driving Ryan to the eye doctor.
Liza Well, how about bike riding? I'm going bike riding on Friday.
Mike I can't. My bike needs new tires.
Liza Oh, all right. I'm going out to buy ice cream. Bye!
Mike Oh, ice cream. I like ice cream.
Liza (*smiling*) Would you like to come?
Mike Would you mind?

E Stress in Compound Nouns

A compound noun is made up of two words: skydiving, ice skating.

▪ In a compound noun, the main stress is usually on the first word.
▪ The second word has a lighter stress.

🎧 Listen and repeat these compound nouns.

bike riding	**sky**diving	**scuba** diving	**ice** skating
hang gliding	**horse**back riding	**ice** cream	**eye** doctor

F Survey

Take a survey. Ask your classmates or other people you know about the activities in the table on the next page. Write their names and answers in the table.

Examples: **A** Have you tried ice skating?   **A** Have you tried skydiving?
       B Yes.   **B** No.
       A Did you like it?   **A** Would you like to try it?
       B No.   **B** Yes.

	Name	Tried it	Liked it	Would like to try it
ice skating				
skydiving				
hiking				
climbing				
kayaking				
horseback riding				
hang gliding				
bike riding				
scuba diving				

G Spelling

The sound /ay/ is usually spelled with the letter *i* or *y*. Add more examples below.

i . . . e fine, like, time, ice, _____
i hi, find, Friday, riding, _____
igh light, tonight, high, _____
y my, why, try, _____
ie tried, lie, die

Unusual spellings: buy, eye, goodbye, height, aisle

H Common Expressions

Listen and repeat these common expressions with the sound /ay/.

Hi.   Good night.
Bye.   I had a nice time.
Why?   I'd like to *try it.

*When /ay/ comes before another vowel sound, use the /y/ sound in /ay/ to link the two vowels together.

/ɔy / • boy

Sentence Rhythm and Timing

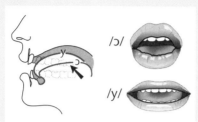

🎧 /ɔy/ has two sounds: /ɔ/ and /y/.
Practice the sound /ɔ/. Make this sound long.
Add /y/ . Make this sound short.
Listen and repeat: /ɔy/.

A Word Pairs

🎧 **1** Listen to these word pairs.

Sound 1: /ɑy/	Sound 2: /ɔy/
buy	boy
ties	toys
pint	point
aisle	oil
file	foil

2 Listen again and repeat.

B Test Yourself

🎧 **1** Listen to the word pairs. Write *S* if the two words are the same or *D* if the two words are different.

1. _____ 2. _____ 3. _____ 4. _____ 5. _____ 6. _____

🎧 **2** Listen to each sentence and circle the word you hear.

1. I slipped and fell in the (aisle / oil).
2. I gave him a (tie / toy) for his birthday.
3. How many (pints / points) did they get?
4. What a good (buy / boy)!
5. I think he's a (liar / lawyer).
6. I put it in the (file / foil).

3 Practice step **2** with a partner. Say each sentence, choosing a word from the word pair. Your partner should point to the word you say.

C Vocabulary

🎧 Listen and repeat these words with the sound /ɔy/.

boys	voices	noisy	annoying
toys	destroy	noisiest	enjoying
noise	spoiled	annoyed	

D Dialog: Noise

Two boys are playing. Their parents are talking about them.

1 Work with a partner. Read the dialog on pages 65 and 66 and circle the correct words in parentheses.

Roy Boys! Stop that noise!

Boys What?

Roy Keep your voices down! You're making too much ((noise)/ noisy)!

Joy Why are you so (annoyed / annoying), Roy? They're just (enjoyed /enjoying) themselves.

Roy But the noise is very (annoyed / annoying).

Joy They're little (boy / boys)–of course they'll make noise.

Roy I'm sure I wasn't that (noisy / noisiest) when I was a little boy. (*raising his voice*) Boys!

Boys (*continue making noise*)

Roy They don't listen. They're spoiled. They (destroy / destroying) all the toys I buy them. And they're the (noisy / noisiest) boys I've ever heard.

Joy Well, maybe you shouldn't buy them such noisy (toy / toys).

Roy It's not the toys that are (noise / noisy) – it's the boys!

🎧 **2** Listen to the dialog and check your answers.

E Sentence Rhythm and Timing

- In English, stressed syllables are longer than unstressed syllables.
- The time it takes to say a sentence depends on the number of stressed syllables, not on the total number of syllables.

🎧 **1** Listen to the sentences on the left.

Kids make noise.	**Buy new toys.**
The **kids make noise.**	**Buy** us **new toys.**
The **kids** will **make noise.**	**Buy** us some **new toys.**
The **kids** are **mak**ing **noise.**	You should **buy** us some **new toys.**
The **kids** have been **mak**ing **noise.**	

2 Listen again and repeat. Try to say all the sentences in the same amount of time. Make the stressed syllables longer and s l o w e r. Make the unstressed syllables shorter and quicker.

3 Now try the sentences on the right.

F Spelling

The sound /ɔy/ is spelled with the letters *oi* or *oy*. Add more examples below.

oi oil, point, voice, noise, _____

oy toy, boy, enjoy, _____

G Common Expressions

🎧 Listen and repeat these common expressions with the sound /ɔy/.

Did you *enj**oy** it?
Please lower your v**oi**ce.

How ann**oy**ing!
What's the p**oi**nt?

*When /ɔy/ comes before another vowel sound, use the /y/ sound in /ɔy/ to link the two vowels together.

/aw/ • house

Stress and Linking in Phrasal Verbs

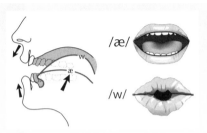

🎧 /aw/ has two sounds: /æ/ and /w/.
Practice the sound /æ/.
Make this sound long.
Add /w/. Make this sound short.
Listen and repeat: /aw/.

A Word Pairs

🎧 **1** Listen to these word pairs.

Sound 1: /ɑ/		Sound 2: /aw/	
	shot	shout	
	Don	down	
R	R	*hour	
	pond	pound	
	moss	mouse	

2 Listen again and repeat.

* Many English speakers add a short /ə/ sound between /aw/ and a following /r/.

B Test Yourself

1 Listen and circle the word you hear.

1. pond / pound   3. R / hour   5. moss / mouse
2. shot / shout   4. Don / down   6. ha! / how

2 Listen to each sentence and circle the word you hear.

1. Did you see the (moss / mouse) in the garden?
2. Is it one (R / hour) or two?
3. Are you going (, Don / down)?
4. The (shots / shouts) woke me.
5. How many (ponds / pounds) are there?
6. ("Ha!" / "How?") he said in surprise.

3 Practice step **2** with a partner. Say each sentence, choosing a word from the word pair. Your partner should point to the word you say.

C Vocabulary

1 One of these words does not have the sound /aw/. Circle this word.

now	around	hour	brown
out	found	shower	couch
town	house	saw	loud

2 Listen. Repeat the words and check your answer.

D Dialog: A mouse in the house

Holly found a mouse in the house.

1 Work with a partner. Read the dialog. Fill in the blanks with the missing words: *down, out,* or *around.*

Holly (*shouting loudly*) There's a mouse in the house!

Howard Ow! Not so loud! Calm __down__! Please stop shouting and sit _____.

Holly (*sitting down*) I found a mouse!

Howard A mouse?

Holly Yes! I was lying _____ on the couch and I heard a sound.

Howard It was probably something outside. Or maybe the shower. I was taking a shower.

Holly No, I saw the mouse! It was a little brown mouse, and it was running _____.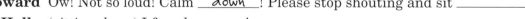

Howard Where is it now?

Holly It's under the couch.

Howard Well, let's get it _____!

Holly How?

Howard (*shouting*) Move the couch _____. Turn it upside _____. We have to get it _____ somehow. We can't have a mouse in the house. We have company coming from _____ of town. They'll be here in an hour!

Holly Calm _____, Howard! Please stop shouting and sit _____! It's just a little brown mouse.

2 Listen to the dialog and check your answers.

E Stress and Linking in Phrasal Verbs

A phrasal verb, or two-word verb, uses a verb + preposition together to create a different meaning from the verb alone.

- In most phrasal verbs, both words are stressed.
- If there is an object pronoun (such as *it*), it is not stressed.
- The words in the phrase are linked together without a break.

1 Listen and repeat.

He's **sit**ting **down**.
He's **ly**ing **down**.
He's **turn**ing a**round**.

He's **go**ing **out**.
He's **run**ning a**round**.
He's **work**ing **out**.

2 Work with a partner. Match each picture with the correct sentence in step **1**.

1.

2.

3.

4.

5.

6.

🎧 **3** Listen and repeat.

Throw it **out**.	**Turn** it **down**.
Put it **down**.	**Cross** it **out**.
Figure it **out**.	**Write** it **down**.

4 Work with a partner. Match each picture with the correct sentence in step **3**.

1.

2.

3.

4.

5.

6.

F Spelling

The sound /aw/ is spelled with the letters *ou* or *ow*. Add more examples below.

ou   about, found, mouth, house, _____

ow   down, crowd, now, how, _____

G Common Expressions

🎧 Listen and repeat these common expressions with the sound /aw/.

Wow!	Please sit **down**.
I f**ou**nd it.	**How** do you pron**ou**nce this?
***How** are you?	I tried to s**ou**nd it **ou**t.

*When /aw/ comes before another vowel sound, use the /w/ sound in /aw/ to link the two vowels together.

Review

/ɑy/, /ɔy/, and /ɑw/

A Test Yourself

1: /ɑy/	2: /ɔy/	3: /ɑw/
buy	boy	bow
aisle	oil	owl
tile	toil	towel
lied	Lloyd	loud

🎧 Listen to words from the table. When you hear a word, write the number of its vowel sound.

1. (boy) 2 _____   4. _____   7. _____
2. _____   5. _____   8. _____
3. _____   6. _____   9. _____

B Linking Practice

When /ɑy/, /ɔy/, or /ɑw/ comes before another vowel sound, use the /y/ or /w/ sound to link it to the following vowel.

🎧 1 Listen to the sentences. Draw a linking line from /ɑy/, /ɔy/, or /ɑw/ to the following vowel. Write /y/ or /w/ above the linking line.

1. Did you buy /y/ it?

2. Now /w/ I see.

3. Why don't you try it?

4. You might enjoy it.

5. How are you doing?

6. Is the boy on the ground?

7. Why is there a cloud?

2 Listen again. Repeat the sentences and check your answers.

C Dialog: A boy lying down

Kyle is painting a picture.

1 Read the dialog. Find at least three more words for each sound in the table. Write the words in the table.

1: /ay/	2: /ɔy/	3: /aw/
lying	boy	down

Troy How are you doing with your painting?
Kyle All right.
Troy Is that a boy?
Kyle Yes. I'm trying to paint a boy lying down.
Troy Is the boy on the ground?
Kyle Yes, he's lying on the ground looking up at the sky.
Troy Hm, now I see. . . . Why don't you try using oil paints?
Kyle I've never tried painting with oils. It sounds hard.
Troy You should buy some oil paints and try it. You might enjoy it.
Kyle I guess you don't like my painting.
Troy It's nice, but why is there a big brown cloud behind the boy?
Kyle (*pointing*) It isn't a cloud. It's a mountain.

2 Listen to the dialog and check your answers.

D Puzzle: Which word doesn't belong?

Circle the word in each line that does not have the same vowel sound as the others.

1. sky   bike   win   nice   time
2. noise   enjoy   foil   hole   point
3. found   throw   hour   crowd   around
4. show   pound   couch   town   shower
5. mind   give   vine   climb   hide
6. destroy spoil   annoy   join   going

Review

The Unstressed Vowels / ə/ and /ər/

A Test Yourself

1 Read the sentences and look at the pictures. Guess the missing words.
The missing words all have the sound /ə/ or /ər/.

She closed __her__ eyes.

She looked _____ _____ clock.

She packed _____ pair _____ binoculars.

_____ brother _____ sister _____ laughing _____ her.

"I'd love _____ go _____ South America."

2 Listen. Repeat the sentences and check your answers.

B Stressed Syllables in Words

In the words below, the spelling has been changed to show you when to use the
sound /ə/ or /ər/.

1 Some English words have strong stress on the last syllable. Listen and
repeat. Make the stressed vowels long and the unstressed vowels short.

be**gin**	de**cide**	hər**self**	re**peat**
ə**gain**	fər**get**	ə'**clock**	aftər**noon**

2 Some words have strong stress in the middle. Listen and repeat.

tə**mor**row	ə**mer**əcə	bə**noc**ulərs (*u* = /yə/)
re**mem**bər	convər**sat**iən	

∩ **3** But most words, especially nouns with two syllables, have strong stress on the first syllable. Listen and repeat.

sistər	**mor**ning	**cam**¢rə	**beau**təfəl
answər	**sev**ən	**com**f∅rtəble	**Sat**ərday
quartər	**break**fəst	**qui**ətly	**pho**təgraph

C Puzzle: Which word doesn't belong?

Circle the word in each line that does not have the same stress pattern as the others. If you are not sure of the stress pattern, try to find a similar word in task B.

1. (yourself)   seven   morning   softly
2. about   open   forget   asleep
3. water   began   better   listen
4. remember   vacation   together   photograph
5. wonderful   comfortable afternoon   quietly
6. decide   picture   breakfast   camera

D Reading: A dream vacation

∩ **1** Cover the story and listen. Look at the sentences and pictures in task A. Number them in the correct order.

2 Listen again and read the story. The spelling has been changed to show you when to use the sound /ə/.

Məriə spent Satərday aftərnoon looking ət ə beautəfəl book əbout South əmerəcə.
"I'd love tə go tə South əmerəcə," she said tə hərself.

Thə next morning, Məriə woke up ət six ə'clock. Hər brothər ənd sistər wəre still əsleep. Məriə looked ət thəm ənd closed hər eyes əgain.

Then she quiətly got out əf bed ənd began tə pack ə suitcase. She packed səme comfərtəble clothes, ə pair əf bənoculərs, ənd hər sistər's camərə. She remembərəd tə take ə hat fər thə sun. She also decidəd tə pack ə photəgraph əf hərself ənd ə pictərə əf hər mothər ənd fathər.

"I'd bettər not fərget tə have səme breakfəst," she said tə hərself. Bət then she looked ət thə clock. It wəs ə quartər tə sevən.

"I don't want tə be late," she said. "I'll just have ə glass əf watər now."

"ə glass əf watər," she said softly. "Watər," she said, ənd opənəd hər eyes.

She wəs still in bed, ənd hər brothər ənd sistər wəre laughing ət hər.

"Tell əs what yə wəre dreaming əbout," they said tə hər.

Bət Məriə didn't answər. She wəs thinking əbout hər wondərfəl trip tə South əmerəcə.

3 Practice reading the story aloud.

/ər/ • word

Tag Questions with Falling Intonation

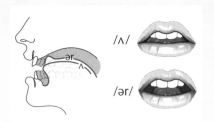

🎧 Practice the sound /ʌ/.
Close your mouth a little.
Curl the tip of your tongue up and back to say /ər/.
The sound /ər/ is pronounced as one sound.
Listen and repeat: /ər/.*

A Word Pairs 1

🎧 **1** Listen to these word pairs.

Sound 1: /ɔr/		Sound 2: /ər/	
	four	fur	
	store	stir	
	torn	turn	
	shorts	shirts	
	award	a word	word

2 Listen again and repeat.

* This is the same sound as /ər/ in Units 9 and 20, but in this unit it is stressed.

Word Pairs 2

🎧 **1** Listen to these word pairs.

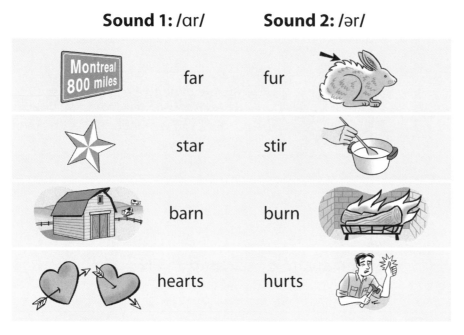

Sound 1: /ɑr/	Sound 2: /ər/
far	fur
star	stir
barn	burn
hearts	hurts

2 Listen again and repeat.

C Word Pairs 3

🎧 **1** Listen to these word pairs.

Sound 1: /ʌ/	Sound 2: /ər/
shut	shirt
bud	bird
bun	burn
gull	girl

2 Listen again and repeat.

D Test Yourself

1 Listen and circle the word you hear.

1. four / far / fur
2. store / star / stir
3. short / shut / shirt
4. bored / bud / bird
5. torn / ton / turn
6. born / barn / bun / burn

2 Listen to each sentence and circle the word you hear.

1. Is it (four / far / fur)?
2. They were wearing black (shorts / shirts).
3. Do you see the (buds / birds) on the tree?
4. Can you (walk / work) faster?
5. Those (barns / buns / burns) don't look good to me.
6. There were two (gulls / girls) on the beach.

3 Practice step **2** with a partner. Say each sentence, choosing a word from the word pair. Your partner should point to the word you say.

E Vocabulary

Listen and repeat these words with the sound /ər/.

nurse	earns	were	dirty	world
hurts	work	weren't	thirty	certainly
heard	first	early	worst	Thursday

F Dialog: The worst nurse

Two patients are talking about the nurses at a hospital.

1 Work with a partner. Read the dialog. Fill in the blanks with words from task E.

Bert Nurse! Nurse! I'm thirsty!

Earl Nurse! My head _____hurts_____!

Bert (*turning to Earl*) Pearl is the _____ nurse, isn't she?

Earl Personally, I think Kurt is worse.

Bert Mmm. He always leaves work _____.

Earl And he always wears a _____ shirt.

Bert I heard he _____ thirty dollars an hour.

Earl He _____ doesn't deserve it.

Bert He and Pearl weren't at work on Thursday, _____ they?

Earl They're the worst nurses on the floor, aren't they?

Bert No – they're the worst nurses in the _____!

2 Listen to the dialog and check your answers.

G Tag Questions with Falling Intonation

A tag question is a question like *isn't she?* or *were they?* added to the end of a sentence.

- A tag question has rising intonation when you want to check information:

  I told you the story, didn't I?
- A tag question has falling intonation when you expect the other person to agree with you.

Listen and repeat these tag questions with falling intonation.

He's the worst **nurse, is**n't he?   They weren't at **work, were** they?

H Conversation Practice

Practice with a partner. Student A adds a tag question to each sentence. Student B responds. Use falling intonation on the tag questions. Listen to these two examples.

You were thirsty.

A You were **thirst**y, **were**n't you?

B Yes, I **was**.

We weren't early.

A We weren't **ear**ly, **were** we?

B No, we **were**n't.

1. You were nervous.
2. You weren't at work.
3. We weren't the worst.
4. The birthday gifts were perfect.
5. The words were hard to learn.
6. You weren't born here.

I Spelling

The sound /ər/ is spelled many different ways. Add more examples below.

er   person, weren't, certainly, prefer, _____

ir   first, bird, girl, circle, _____

ur   Thursday, nurse, hurt, turn, _____

Other spellings:

or   after the letter *w*: word, work, world, worst

ear   early, learn, heard, earth

J Common Expressions

Listen and repeat these common expressions with the sound /ər/.

Hurry!   I walk to w**or**k.

C**er**tainly.   I was the **fir**st p**er**son there.

Don't w**or**ry.   the w**or**ld's w**or**st

Section B
CONSONANTS

Making Consonant

Match these words with the
numbers in the pictures.

- a. nose
- b. top teeth
- c. top lip
- d. tongue
- e. bottom teeth
- f. bottom lip

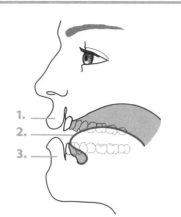

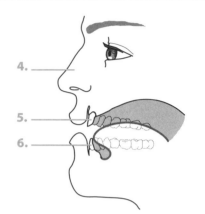

Match these words with the
numbers in the pictures.

- a. the back of the tongue
- b. the roof of the mouth
- c. the tip of the tongue
- d. the side teeth
- e. the front of the tongue
- f. the sides of the tongue

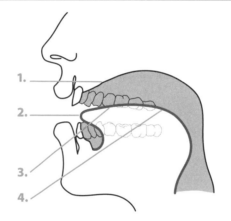

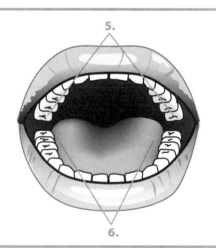

Practice using air to make consonant sounds.

1. Hold a piece of
paper in front
of your mouth.

2. When you blow
out air, the
paper moves.

3. Air is coming
through your
mouth.

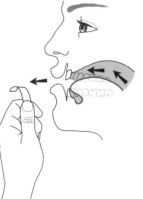

The pictures below show how to make the sounds /p/ (as in *paper*),
/t/ (as in *tea*), and /k/ (as in *key*). Practice saying /p/, /t/, and /k/.

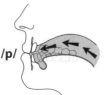

/p/

1. Close your lips.

   Push air forward
   in your mouth.

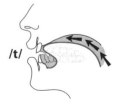

/t/

2. Touch the front of the roof
of your mouth with the tip
of your tongue.

   Push air forward in your mouth.

Sounds

Practice moving your lips.

1. Open your lips.

2. Close your lips.

3. Close your lips tight.

4. Make your lips round.

Practice moving your tongue.

1. Touch:
   – your top teeth
   – your bottom teeth
   – the roof of your mouth with your tongue.

2. Touch your side teeth with the sides of your tongue.

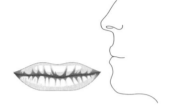

3. Touch the front of the roof of your mouth with the front of your tongue.

4. Touch the back of the roof of your mouth with the back of your tongue.

Practice using your voice.

1. Put your hand on the front of your neck.

2. When you sing, you can feel your voice. You are using your voice.

3. The sound of your voice is coming through your mouth.

4. Use your voice to make some consonant sounds (such as /b/, /z/, /m/, and /l/). Do not use your voice to make other consonant sounds (such as /p/, /s/, and /h/).

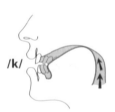

3. Touch the back of the roof of your mouth with the back of your tongue.

Push air forward in your mouth.

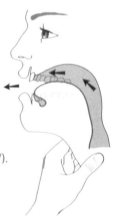

UNIT 22 /p/ • pop

Intonation in Lists

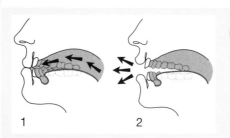

🎧 Close your lips tight.
Push air forward in your mouth.
Open your lips quickly.
Do not use your voice.
Listen and repeat: /p/.

A Vocabulary

🎧 **1** At the beginning of a word or a stressed syllable, say /p/ with a strong puff of air. Listen and repeat.

a pen	a pencil	passports
pictures	presents	a CD player
a paper plate	a piece of pie	a pillow
a plastic bag	toothpaste	a newspaper

🎧 **2** The sound /p/ is quieter in these words. It does not have a strong puff of air. Listen and repeat.

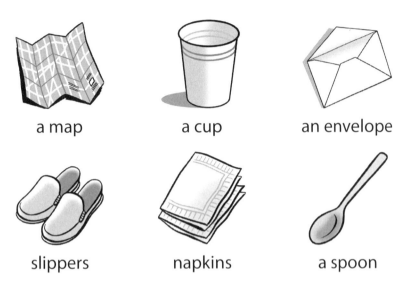

| a map | a cup | an envelope |

| slippers | napkins | a spoon |

🎧 **3** Listen and repeat. Underline the /p/ sounds that are pronounced with a strong puff of air.

a purse   a postcard   a laptop   stamps   pennies   an apple

B **Dialog:** "Passports, please"

Peter and Pam are at the airport. They just arrived from Paris.

🎧 **1** Cover the dialog and listen. Check ✓ the items in task A that Peter and Pam packed.

2 Listen again and read the dialog. Check your answers to step **1**.

Official Passports, please.

Pam Peter? Aren't the passports in your pocket?

Peter I thought you put them in your purse, Pam.

Pam (*inspecting her purse*) No. I have a pen, a postcard, a map, a spoon, and some pictures. Check your pocket.

Peter (*emptying his pocket*) I have a pencil, some stamps, an envelope, some pennies . . .

Pam Please stop taking everything out of your pocket. You probably put them in the plastic bag.

Peter (*emptying the plastic bag*) Here's a cup, an apple, a paper plate, some presents, a newspaper . . .

Pam Peter, stop pulling everything out of the plastic bag! People are getting impatient.

Peter Please help me. Help put the things back in the plastic bag.

Pam (*speaking to the official*) We have a problem. We can't find our passports.

Official Let the other passengers past, please.

Peter It's possible we dropped them on the plane.

Official Please go upstairs with this police officer.

C Intonation in Lists

- In saying a list of items, the intonation often rises on each item before the last item.
- On the last item, the intonation falls to a low note to show that the list is finished.

1 Listen to these lists. They are not finished. The stressed words and syllables are in **bold**.

I have a **pen**cil, some **stamps**, an **en**velope, some **pen**nies . . .

Here's a **cup**, an **ap**ple, a **pa**per **plate**, some **pres**ents, a **news**paper . . .

2 Listen to this list. It is finished.

I have a **pen**, a **post**card, a **map**, a **spoon**, and some **pic**tures.

D Conversation Practice

Which items in task A do you usually pack when you travel? Practice this conversation with a partner. Replace the underlined items with items from task A.

A What do you usually pack when you travel?

B I usually pack a passport, a pen, toothpaste, slippers, and a laptop.

E Game: "The perfect picnic"

Play this game with the whole class. Choose words from the list on the next page. Each person adds something new.

Example: **A** We're having a picnic, and I'm bringing pears.

B We're having a picnic. **A** is bringing pears, and I'm bringing potato chips.

C We're having a picnic. **A** is bringing pears, **B** is bringing potato chips, and I'm bringing soup.

apples	**pas**ta	**pa**per **plates**
pears	**pep**per	**plas**tic **cups**
po**ta**to chips	**pie**	**nap**kins
popcorn	**soup**	a **CD** player
pizza	**spoons**	a **pic**nic basket

F Spelling

The sound /p/ is spelled with the letter *p*. Add more examples below.

p   paper, people, envelope, stamp, _____

pp happy, pepper, shopping, dropped, _____

Careful: The letter *p* is silent in these words: p̶sychology, p̶neumonia, receip̶t, cup̶board.

G Common Expressions

🎧 Listen and repeat these common expressions with the sound /p/.

Please hel**p**.	Oo**ps**! I dro**pp**ed it.
Sto**p p**ushing!*	**P**ick it u**p**.
It's **p**retty im**p**ortant.	**P**lease **p**ass the **pep**per.

*When /p/ comes before another /p/, pronounce the two /p/ sounds as one long /p/. Do not say two separate /p/ sounds.

UNIT 23

/b/ • baby

Stress in Compound Nouns and Phrases

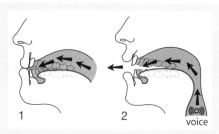

🎧 Practice the sound /p/.
Use your voice to say /b/.
Listen and repeat: /b/.

1   2   voice

A Word Pairs

🎧 **1** Listen to these word pairs.

Sound 1: /p/		Sound 2: /b/	
	pie	buy	
	pear	bear	
	pill	bill	
	cap	cab	
	rope	robe	

2 Listen again and repeat.

B Test Yourself

1 Listen to the word pairs. Write *S* if the two words are the same or *D* if the two words are different.

1. _____ 2. _____ 3. _____ 4. _____ 5. _____ 6. _____

2 Listen to each sentence and circle the word you hear.

1. She threw away her old (pills / bills).
2. It was a little (pig / big).
3. What color was the (cap / cab)?
4. There are (pears / bears) in the garden.
5. I put the (rope / robe) in the closet.
6. Could you tell me where the (path / bath) is?

3 Practice step **2** with a partner. Say each sentence, choosing a word from the word pair. Your partner should point to the word you say.

C Vocabulary

1 Listen and repeat these words with the sound /b/.

a bookshelf	a birthday cake	blue beads
a backpack	paintbrushes	a beautiful bracelet
a cookbook	a black box	October

2 Work with a partner. Match the pictures with the words in step **1**.

1. 2. 3. 4. 5.

6. 7. 8. 9.

3 The sound /b/ is quiet at the end of a word. The vowel before it is long. Listen and repeat.

a cab   a job   a bathrobe   a club

D Dialog: "Happy birthday!"

Today is Barbara's birthday.

🎧 **1** Read the dialog as you listen. If you hear a word that is different from the word in your book, correct the word. Use the words in task C. There are eight words to correct. The first one has been done for you.

Bob Hi, Barbara. You look happy.

Barbara (*pause*) Well . . . you know, today's my birthday.

Bob Oh, right, ~~December~~ <u>October</u> 7th. Your birthday! Happy birthday!

Barbara Thanks, Bob. Look at this box Abby gave me. I can't believe she made it.

Bob Yeah, those black beads are beautiful. (*pause*) Is that a new backpack? Was that a birthday present, too?

Barbara The backpack? No, I bought it myself.

Bob What did your parents give you for your birthday?

Barbara A set of golf clubs. And my Mom baked a birthday cake.

Bob What about your brother? Did he give you anything?

Barbara Yes, he built a table for my bedroom. And, uh, somebody gave me a bathrobe.

Bob I'm really sorry, Barbara, but I totally forgot about your birthday. I've been so busy with my boat.

Barbara Well, my birthday isn't over yet . . .

Bob Right! Let's go out and celebrate. How about taking a cab to that new bookstore?

2 Listen again and check your answers.

E Stress in Compound Nouns and Phrases

- In a compound noun, the main stress is usually on the first word.
- In an ordinary noun phrase with an adjective + a noun, the main stress is usually on the last word – the noun.

🎧 **1** Listen and repeat these compound nouns.

    a **cook**book   a **book**shelf   a **birth**day cake

🎧 **2** Listen and repeat these noun phrases.

a black **box**   blue **beads**   a beautiful **brace**let

F Conversation Practice

1 Work with a partner. Use the words below to make a compound noun or phrase for each picture. Underline the stressed word or syllable.

black	cook	cowboy	rubber
tea	funny	sleeping	big

1. a <u>cook</u>book

2. a _____ pot

3. a _____ bag

4. a _____ pot

5. a _____ book

6. _____ boots

7. a _____ bag

8. _____ boots

🎧 **2** Listen. Repeat the words and check your answers.

3 Practice this conversation with a partner. Replace the underlined items with compound nouns or noun phrases from this unit.

A What should we get Barbara for her birthday?
B How about <u>a backpack</u>?
A I have a better idea. How about <u>a funny book</u>?

G Spelling

The sound /b/ is spelled with the letter *b*. Add more examples below.

b   birthday, about, table, job, _____
bb   rubber, robber, grabbed

Careful: The letter *b* is silent in these words: clim~~b~~, lam~~b~~, thum~~b~~, com~~b~~, bom~~b~~, dou~~b~~t, de~~b~~t.

H Common Expressions

🎧 Listen and repeat these common expressions with the sound /b/.

Happy **b**irthday!   I **b**ought a **b**ook.
I'll **b**e right **b**ack.   It's a **b**ig jo**b**.
I've **b**een **b**usy.   Is there a pro**b**lem?

UNIT 24

/t/ • two

Linking a Final Consonant

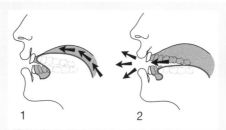

🎧 Put your tongue just behind your top teeth.
Your tongue should not touch your teeth.
Push air forward in your mouth.
Then quickly move your tongue away.
Do not use your voice.
Listen and repeat: /t/.

A Vocabulary

🎧 **1** At the beginning of a word or a stressed syllable, say /t/ with a strong puff of air. Listen and repeat.

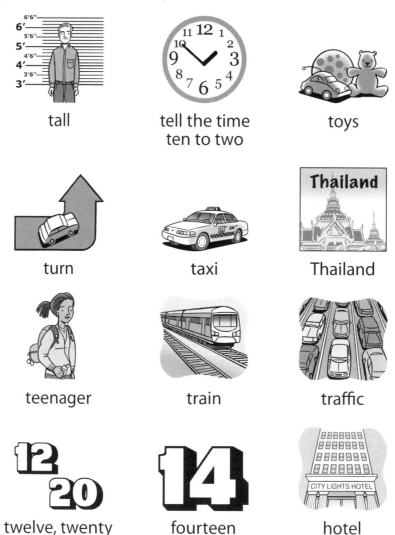

tall

tell the time
ten to two

toys

turn

taxi

Thailand

teenager

train

traffic

twelve, twenty

fourteen

hotel

🎧 **2** After /s/, the sound /t/ does not have a strong puff of air. Listen and repeat.

station   stamps   store

street   restaurant   taxi stand

🎧 **3** At the end of a word or syllable, /t/ is quiet. Listen and repeat.

right	short	can't	exactly
great	left	light	best bet

🎧 **4** In American English, /t/ is "flapped" – pronounced like a quick /d/ – when it comes after a vowel and before an unstressed vowel. Listen and repeat.

water   computer   letter   visitor   city   hospital

B Dialog: At the visitor center

People at the visitor center are asking a staff member some questions.

🎧 **1** Listen to the dialog while you look at the map. Match the places listed on the right with the numbers on the map. Which place is *not* on the map?

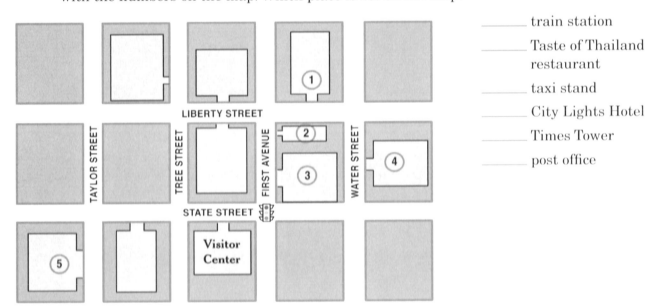

_____ train station

_____ Taste of Thailand restaurant

_____ taxi stand

_____ City Lights Hotel

_____ Times Tower

_____ post office

2 Listen again and read the dialog. Check your answers to step **1**.

Tall woman Could you tell me how to get to the train station?

Staff member The train station? Turn right when you leave the visitor center. When you get to the light, turn left onto First Avenue. The train station will be on your right. You can't miss it.

Student Are there any Thai restaurants around here?

Staff member Thai restaurants? There's a great Thai restaurant on Water Street. It's called Taste of Thailand. Go two blocks to the right and then left onto Water Street.

Tall man Where can I get a taxi?

Staff member Try the taxi stand on First Avenue. Just go to the right and turn left at the light. It's just past the train station.

Tired tourist How do I get to the City Lights Hotel?

Staff member Go two blocks to the right and turn left on Water Street. Then turn left again when you get to Liberty Street. You'll see a tall white building. That's it.

Teenage girl I'm trying to get to the Times Tower.

Staff member Well, you can take the number 12 bus – it stops right outside the visitor center – and get off at 14th Street. But it might be better to walk. There's a lot of traffic this time of day.

Short woman Where can I get stamps for these letters?

Staff member Your best bet is the post office. When you go out of here, turn that way (*pointing left*). Go two blocks. Then turn left onto Taylor Street. It'll be on your right.

Little girl Do you know what time it is?

Staff member It's exactly twenty-two minutes after ten.

C Linking a Final Consonant

In speech, words are linked together without a break. Link a final consonant (a consonant at the end of a word) to the sound at the beginning of the next word.

- final consonant + a vowel: Link the final consonant smoothly to a vowel. Pronounce the consonant as part of the next word.
- vowel /t/ + a vowel: If final /t/ comes after a vowel and before another vowel, the /t/ is "flapped." Pronounce the /t/ like a quick /d/.
- final consonant + the same consonant: Pronounce the two consonants as one long consonant sound. Do not say two separate sounds.
- final consonant + a different consonant: Say the final consonant quietly. Go right to the next sound.

🎧 **1** Listen and repeat. Link the final /t/ to the following vowel.

post office   First Avenue

🎧 **2** Listen and repeat. The /t/ sound is flapped here.

a lot of   get off

🎧 **3** Listen and repeat. Pronounce the linked /t/ sounds as one long /t/.

a great Thai restaurant   What time is it?

🎧 **4** Listen and repeat. Make the /t/ sound quiet before the next consonant.

your best bet   just past

D Conversation Practice

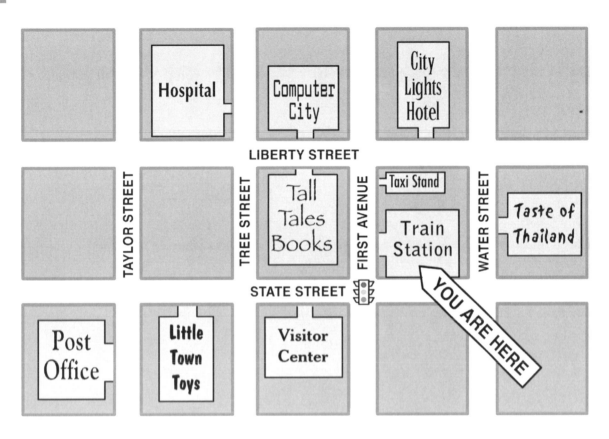

1 Read the dialog on page 92 again.

2 Practice with a partner. One person asks for directions from the train station to these places.

the visitor center	the hospital
the City Lights Hotel	Little Town Toys
the post office	Computer City
the Taste of Thailand restaurant	Tall Tales bookstore

Ask questions like these:

Could you tell me how to get to _____?

How do I get to _____?

The other person answers, using the map on page 93.

E Spelling

The sound /t/ is usually spelled with the letter *t*. Add more examples below.

t   time, try, twelve, city, _____

tt   letter, matter, little, getting

Unusual spellings: look<u>ed</u>, miss<u>ed</u>, <u>Th</u>ailand

Careful: The letter *t* is silent in these words: lis~~t~~en, of~~t~~en, whis~~t~~le, cas~~t~~le, Chris~~t~~mas, balle~~t~~.

F Common Expressions

Listen and repeat these common expressions with the sound /t/.

What **t**ime is it?	Just a minu**t**e.
What's the ma**tt**er?	Could you **t**ell me how **t**o ge**t** **t**o the **t**rain station?
Take it easy!	Thanks! It's no **t**rouble at all.

UNIT 25

/d/ • did

-ed Endings

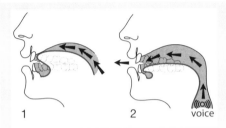

🎧 Practice the sound /t/.
Use your voice to say /d/.
Listen and repeat: /d/.

A Word Pairs

🎧 **1** Listen to these word pairs.

Sound 1: /t/	Sound 2: /d/
time	dime
tore	door
try	dry
write	ride
cart	card

2 Listen again and repeat.

🎧 **1** Listen and circle the word you hear.

1. tore / door	3. try / dry	5. cart / card
2. time / dime	4. write / ride	6. seats / seeds

🎧 **2** Listen to each sentence and circle the word you hear.

1. Do you have the (time / dime)?

2. I want to (try / dry) this shirt.

3. I'll give you my (cart / card).

4. She (writes / rides) very well.

5. Are there any (seats / seeds) left?

6. We (sent / send) all the packages on Monday.

3 Practice step **2** with a partner. Say each sentence, choosing a word from the word pair. Your partner should point to the word you say.

C Vocabulary

🎧 Listen and repeat these words and phrases with the sound /d/.

studied	listened to CDs	cooked a big dinner
played cards	watched a DVD	repaired the phone
cleaned her bedroom	called David	decided to stay home
washed windows	visited a friend	heated up some food

D Dialog: A missed date

David and Diana had plans to get together yesterday.

🎧 **1** Cover the dialog and listen. Then answer the question using words and phrases from task C.

> What did Diana do yesterday?

2 Listen again and read the dialog. Check your answer to step **1**.

Diana (*phone rings*) Hello.

David Hello, Diana? This is David.

Diana Oh, hi, David.

David What happened yesterday? I waited and waited for you. You forgot our date, didn't you?

Diana No, I remembered. But it rained all day and I had a bad cold, so I decided to stay home.

David You did? But I tried to call you at least 20 times and nobody answered!

Diana Oh, the phone lines were damaged by the storm. They repaired them today.

David Oh. And what did your sister Maddy do yesterday? Did she and her boyfriend go dancing?

Diana No, they didn't. They stayed home and played cards.

David And what did you do? Did you play cards, too?

Diana No, I studied and listened to CDs. And after dinner, I watched a DVD with Maddy.

David What did you do for dinner?

Diana I didn't feel like making a big dinner, so I just heated up some frozen food. What did you do yesterday, David?

David I just told you, Diana. I tried to call you 20 times!

E *-ed* Endings

The *-ed* ending is added to verbs to show the past tense.

- The *-ed* ending has three different pronunciations: /t/, /d/, and /əd/.
- The pronunciation of the *-ed* ending depends on the sound that comes before it in the verb.

1 Listen and repeat.

-ed = /t/	-ed = /d/	-ed = /əd/
washed	listened	waited
cooked	studied	decided

2 Listen to the pronunciation of the *-ed* ending in these verbs. Write each verb in the correct column above.

called	played	cleaned	worked	stayed
watched	tried	answered	missed	started
wanted	visited	talked	needed	stopped

3 Listen again. Repeat the words and check your answers to step **2**.

4 Complete these rules.

- The -*ed* ending is pronounced as an extra syllable /əd/ after the sound /____/ or /____/.
- The -*ed* ending is pronounced /____/ after sounds made using the voice (/b, g, z, ʒ, ʤ, v, ð, m, n, ŋ, l, r/, and vowels).
- The -*ed* ending is pronounced /____/ after sounds made *without* using the voice (/p, k, s, ʃ, ʧ, f, θ/).

F Game: "Did I or didn't I?"

1 Write three sentences about what you did or didn't do last weekend. Write two sentences that are true and one that is *not* true. Use verbs from this unit or other past tense verbs.

Example: I worked on Saturday.
I didn't see any movies.
I visited my cousin on Sunday.

2 Practice in a group of three to five people. Take turns saying your sentences. The other people guess which sentences are true and which sentence is false.

G Spelling

The sound /d/ is spelled with the letter *d*. Add more examples below.

d   door, date, didn't, studied, _____

dd address, middle, add, suddenly

Careful: The letter *d* is silent in these words: Wednesday, handsome, handkerchief.

H Common Expressions

🎧 Listen and repeat these common expressions with the sound /d/.

What **d**o you **d**o?   I **d**i**d**n't **d**o it.
That's a goo**d** i**d**ea!   What's to**d**ay's **d**ate?
I **d**on't un**d**erstan**d**.   What's your a**dd**ress?

/k/ • key

Stress in Noun Phrases with Compounds

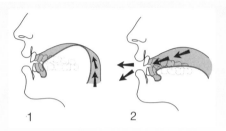

🎧 Touch the back of the roof of your mouth
with the back of your tongue.
Push air forward in your mouth and
quickly move your tongue away.
Do not use your voice.
Listen and repeat: /k/.

1   2

A Vocabulary

🎧 **1** At the beginning of a word or a stressed syllable, say /k/ with a strong
puff of air. Listen and repeat.

cook   kitchen   Canada

clean   cuckoo clock   bookcase

🎧 **2** The sound /k/ is quieter in these words. Listen and repeat.

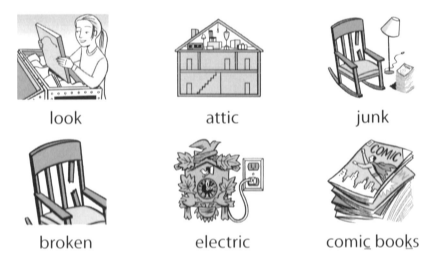

look   attic   junk

broken   electric   comic books

🎧 **3** The sound /k/ comes before another consonant sound in these words. Listen and repeat.

/ ks /	/ kt /	/ kw /
six	collect	quiet
next	perfect	question
expensive	connect	
extra	exactly	
excuse me		

B Dialog: Junk or keepsakes?

Kate and Chris are cleaning out the attic in their house.

1 Work with a partner. Read the dialog. Fill in the blanks with words from task A.

Chris (*climbing up to the attic*) Yikes! _____Look_____ at all this junk. What's in that box? Can you check?

Kate Just a second. . . . Cool, my old _____!

Chris OK, they can go in recycling.

Kate Recycling? No, I can sell them. People _____ old comic books.

Chris Can you take a look at that rocking chair? It looks like the back is _____.

Kate I can fix it, I think. We could use an extra –

Chris Excuse me, what's that _____ to the bookcase? Is that a clock?

Kate It's a cuckoo clock. I got it in _____.

Chris Can I ask you a _____? Why are you keeping a plastic cuckoo clock?

Kate It isn't plastic. It's oak. Actually, it was kind of _____.

Chris Does it work? It's exactly _____ o'clock now, and it's very quiet.

Kate Of course it works. Here, let me connect it. It's _____.
(CUCKOO, CUCKOO, CUCKOO, CUCKOO, CUCKOO)

Kate It would be perfect for the _____, don't you think?

Chris Are you kidding? Listen to that while I cook? I'd go crazy!
(CUCKOO!)

Chris Hey, where are you taking all that _____? Bring it back to the attic!

Kate Junk? You call this junk? These are keepsakes!

🎧 **2** Listen to the dialog and check your answers.

C Stress in Noun Phrases with Compounds

- In an ordinary noun phrase with an adjective + a noun, the main stress is usually on the last word – the noun.
- If a noun phrase contains an adjective and a compound noun, the main stress is on the first part of the compound noun.

🎧 Listen and repeat.

a broken **chair**　　　　a broken **rock**ing chair
an electric **clock**　　　an electric **cuck**oo clock
some old **books**　　　　some old **com**ic books

D Scrambled Phrases

What other things did Kate and Chris find in the attic?

1 Work with a partner. Unscramble the phrases below. Then underline the word or syllable with the strongest stress.

2 Match the phrases to the pictures.

1. ring plastic a key _____ *a plastic <u>key</u> ring* _____

2. cup a coffee black _____

3. can empty cola an _____

4. card an credit expired _____

5. an opener can electric _____

6. ski pink a jacket _____

7. broken box music a _____

8. tickets old some concert _____

9. picture an expensive book _____

E Spelling

The sound /k/ is usually spelled with the letters *k, c,* or *ck*. Add more examples below.

k	key, kitchen, think, walk, like, _____
c	call, electric, collect, crazy, _____
ck	back, clock, jacket, _____
cc	occur, accountant, occasion
	pronounced /ks/ before *e* or *i*: success, accent, accident

Other spellings:

ch	school, chemistry, stomach, headache, Christmas
x, xc	pronounced /ks/: six, next, extra, expensive, excellent, exciting
qu	usually pronounced /kw/: question, quiet, quickly

Careful: The letter *k* is silent before *n* at the beginning of a word: know, knife, knee.

F Common Expressions

Listen and repeat these common expressions with the sound /k/.

Excuse me.	**C**an you **k**eep a se**c**ret?
Come in.	**C**an I **c**all you ba**ck**?
Thanks for **c**alling.	**C**an I as**k** a **qu**estion?

/g/ • good
Gonna (*going to*)

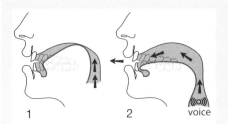

🎧 Practice the sound /k/.
Use your voice to say /g/.
Listen and repeat: /g/.

1   2   voice

A Word Pairs

🎧 **1** Listen to these word pairs.

Sound 1: /k/	Sound 2: /g/
coat	goat
curl	girl
class	glass
back	bag
clock	clog

2 Listen again and repeat.

B Test Yourself

🎧 **1** Listen and circle the word you hear.

1. coat / goat   3. curl / girl   5. clock / clog

2. class / glass   4. cold / gold   6. back / bag

🎧 **2** Listen to each sentence and circle the word you hear.

1. Is that really (cold / gold)?

2. There's a fly on your (back / bag).

3. He has a white (coat / goat).

4. Does the store sell (clocks / clogs)?

5. Those (curls / girls) look nice.

6. How many (classes / glasses) do you have?

3 Practice step **2** with a partner. Say each sentence, choosing a word from the word pair. Your partner should point to the word you say.

C Vocabulary

1 One word in each column does *not* have the sound /g/. Work with a partner. Circle the words that do not have the sound /g/.

good	guitar	beginning	sang
guess	August	message	big
long	again	get	dog
glad	coming	Chicago	together
great	jogging	England	exactly

🎧 **2** Listen. Repeat the words and check your answers.

D Dialog: Guests in August

Friends are planning to visit Gary and Grace in August.

🎧 **1** Listen to the dialog. Circle all the correct words in parentheses.

AUGUST						
2	3	4	5	6 Maggie and Greg	7
9	10	11	12	13	14

1. Gary and Grace live in (Chicago / Michigan / England).

2. Their guests, Maggie and Greg, live in (Chicago / Michigan / England / Canada).

3. Gary and Grace plan to (go jogging / play the guitar / go to a baseball game / play golf / shop for gifts / go to art galleries / go camping) with their guests.

4. After they visit Chicago, Maggie and Greg are going to (Michigan / Canada / Greece).

2 Listen again and read the dialog. Check your answer to step **1**.

> **Gary** Guess who's coming to Chicago?
> **Grace** Maggie and Greg?
> **Gary** How'd you guess? I just got a message from Greg.
> **Grace** Great! When are they going to be in Chicago?
> **Gary** The beginning of August.
> **Grace** I'm glad they're coming in August. Maybe we can get tickets to a baseball game.
> **Gary** Good idea. And Greg and I can play some golf.
> **Grace** Maggie and I can take the dog and go jogging in the park. If the weather's good, maybe we can go swimming in Lake Michigan. And –
> **Gary** They're not going to be here that long. After Chicago, they're going to Canada.
> **Grace** Where in Canada are they going?
> **Gary** I don't know exactly. They're going to go camping.
> **Grace** Remember the big party they gave when we were in England?
> **Gary** How could I forget? Maggie played the guitar with that group.
> **Grace** And we all sat on the grass and sang songs.
> **Gary** I had a great time. It'll be good to get together again.

E Gonna (*going to*)

- In informal speech, *going to* is often pronounced "gonna" when it is used with another verb to show the future.
- Do not use the "gonna" pronunciation when *going* is a main verb.

🎧 Listen and repeat.

> When are they going to ("gonna") be in Chicago?
> They're going to ("gonna") go camping.
> They're going to Canada.

F Conversation Practice

🎧 **1** Listen. Which lines use the "gonna" pronunciation?

> **A** Where are you going for vacation?
> **B** I'm going to England.
> **A** What are you going to do in England?
> **B** I'm going to go to art galleries.

2 Practice the conversation with a partner. Replace the underlined items with the place names and activities below.

> **A** Where are you going for vacation?
> **B** I'm going to England.
> **A** What are you going to do in England?
> **B** I'm going to go to art galleries.

England	play golf
Greece	go jogging
Portugal	go to a baseball (*or* soccer) game
Chicago	go to art galleries
Las Vegas	shop for gifts
Niagara Falls	take a lot of photographs
the Grand Canyon	practice speaking English (*or* Greek *or* . . .)

G Spelling

The sound /g/ is usually spelled with the letter *g*. Add more examples below.

> **g**   garden, grass, again, dog, _____
> **gg** jogging, bigger, egg
> **gu** guest, guess, guitar

Other spellings:

> **gh** ghost, spaghetti
> **x**   pronounced /gz/: example, exactly, exam, exit

Careful: The letter *g* is silent in these words: sign, foreign, designer, right, night, thought, daughter, neighbor.

H Common Expressions

Listen and repeat these common expressions with the sound /g/.

Great!	**G**ood to see you a**g**ain.
Let's **g**et to**g**ether.	I've **g**ot to **g**o.
Give me a call.	What are you **g**oing to ("**g**onna") do?

UNIT 28

Review
/p/, /b/, /t/, /d/, /k/, and /g/

A Test Yourself

🎧 **1** Listen and circle the word you hear. You can use a dictionary if you like, but you don't have to understand every word to do this.

1. pack / back / bag	7. pet / bet / bed
2. pick / pig / big	8. coat / code / goat / goad
3. colt / cold / gold	9. tuck / tug / duck / dug
4. plant / planned / bland	10. pat / pad / bat / bad
5. cart / card / guard	11. puck / pug / buck / bug
6. tap / tab / dab	12. cap / cab / gap / gab

2 Complete the rules with the correct symbols: /p/, /b/, /t/, /d/, /k/, or /g/. Listen to the words in step **1** again if you need to.

- The consonant sounds /_____/, /_____/, and /_____/ are pronounced with a strong puff of air at the beginning of a word or stressed syllable.
- Vowel sounds are longer when they come before the consonant sound /_____/, /_____/, or /_____/ at the end of a word.

B Vocabulary

1 In each item underline the syllable that has the strongest stress.

kitchen	cake plates
potato chips	chocolate ice cream
cold drinks	a paper tablecloth
plastic cups	an extra table
a baking pan	her electric guitar

🎧 **2** Listen. Repeat the words and check your answers.

🎧 **3** Karen is planning a party. Listen to the list of things she needs to do.

To Do List

☑ **To Do List**

- ☐ Clean the kitchen!
- ☐ Buy:
- ☐   Potato chips
- ☐   cold drinks
- ☐   plastic cups
- ☐   cake plates
- ☐   chocolate ice cream
- ☐   a paper tablecloth
- ☐ Call Ted. Ask him to bring an extra table.
- ☐ Ask Kate to bring her electric guitar.
- ☐

4 Practice reading Karen's To Do List aloud. Use rising intonation on each item before the last item in the list of things she needs to buy. Use falling intonation on the last item.

5 Think of something you are planning. Write a To Do List. Then read it aloud.

C   Puzzle: Which word doesn't belong?

Circle the -ed ending in each line that does not have the same sound as the others.

1. walked   watched   laughed   (called)
2. visited   asked   waited   needed
3. listened   cleaned   rented   rained
4. painted   answered   played   tried
5. helped   missed   danced   decided
6. pushed   snowed   stayed   happened

UNIT 29

/s/ • sun

Linking a Final Consonant Cluster

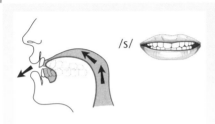

/s/

🎧 Touch your top teeth
with the sides of your tongue.
Put your tongue forward, behind your top teeth.
Force air out over the top of your tongue.
Do not use your voice.
Listen and repeat: /s/.

A Vocabulary

🎧 **1** Listen and repeat.

sailing   surfing   sitting on the sand

seashore   Saturday   Sunday

🎧 **2** /s/ often occurs in consonant clusters, or groups of consonant sounds.
Listen and repeat.*

swimming   waterskiing   skating

sleep outside   stay in a hotel   star

*Careful: Do not add an extra vowel sound before or after /s/ in a consonant cluster.

3 Listen and repeat. Circle the words that have the consonant clusters: /sp/, /ts/, or /ks/.

silly	exciting	six
excellent	that's	serious
sports	sensible	expensive

B Dialog: It's expensive

Six Star Hotel

Stacy and Steve are planning a trip to the seashore.

1 Cover the dialog and listen. Circle the correct words in parentheses.

1. Stacy likes (skating / waterskiing).
2. Steve wants to (save / spend) money.
3. Stacy wants to stay over (Saturday / Sunday) night.
4. Stacy thinks sleeping outside is (sensible / exciting).

2 Listen again and read the dialog. Check your answers to step **1**.

Steve   Let's go to the seashore on Saturday.
Stacy   Yes! Excellent! Would you rather go sailing or waterskiing? Waterskiing is so exciting.
Steve   It's also expensive, Stacy. Let's just sit in the sun and go swimming instead.
Stacy   Let's stay over Saturday night and spend Sunday there, too. We could stay at the Six Star Hotel.
Steve   Be sensible, Sweetie. It's too expensive. Let's sleep outside instead.
Stacy   Yes. Let's sleep on the sand. That's more exciting.

C Linking a Final Consonant Cluster

Adding the ending -*s* to a word often creates a consonant cluster: for example, *likes* (/ks/), *wants* (/nts/), *it's* (/ts/).

- /s/ + a vowel: If the next word begins with a vowel sound, link the final /s/ clearly to the vowel.
- /s/ + /s/ : If the next word begins with /s/, say the two /s/ sounds as one long /s/. Do not say two separate /s/ sounds.
- Careful: Do not drop -*s* at the end of a word.

1 Listen and repeat. Link /s/ to the following vowel.

It's expensive.
Let's eat.

🎧 **2** Listen and repeat. Pronounce the linked /s/ sounds as one long /s/.

> Let's sit.
> Let's sit on the sand.
> Let's stay in a hotel.
> Let's sleep outside.

D Scrambled Conversations

1 Practice with a partner. Student A says a sentence on the left. Student B responds with a sentence from the right.

A	**B**
Let's sit in the sun.	Let's sleep outside instead.
Let's eat steak.	Let's swim in the pool instead.
Let's stay in a hotel.	Let's sit in the shade instead.
Let's spend all the money.	Let's ask Steve instead.
Let's swim in the ocean.	Let's speak English instead.
Let's see a movie on Sunday.	Let's save some money instead.
Let's ask Stacy.	Let's study on Sunday instead.
Let's speak Spanish.	Let's eat pizza instead.

🎧 **2** Listen and check your answers.

E Interview: Personality test

Work with a partner. Do you like to take risks or are you more cautious? Try this personality test for fun.

🎧 **1** Listen. Notice the intonation in the question: rising on the first choice (before *or*) and falling on the second choice (after *or*).

> **A** Would you rather sleep out**side** or stay in a ho**tel**?
> **B** Sleep outside.

2 Interview your partner. For each question, give 1 point if your partner chooses the first item and 0 points if your partner chooses the second item. Then change roles. Begin your questions with this phrase:

> Would you rather . . .

1. sleep outside or stay in a hotel?
2. spend money or save money?
3. play sports or watch sports?
4. drive fast or slowly?
5. be a movie star or a dentist?
6. go surfing or sit on the sand?
7. go swimming on Saturday morning or sleep late?
8. be silly or serious?
9. eat something spicy or sweet?
10. ask a question or answer a question?
11. do something exciting or relaxing?

3 Add up your partner's points, and tell your partner the results.

9–11 points: You are very adventurous – maybe too adventurous? Slow down a little!

5–8 points: You like excitement, but you try to stay safe.

1–4 points: You are serious and cautious – maybe too cautious? Try relaxing a little!

F Spelling

The sound /s/ is usually written with the letter *s* or *c*. Add more examples below.

s	sun, stop, yes, serious, _____
ss	class, address, kiss, possible
c	before *e, i,* or *y*: notice, cent, city, bicycle, _____
se	house, horse, promise, close (adjective)

Other spellings:

sc	science, scene, scissors, muscle
x, xc	pronounced /ks/: six, expensive, next, exciting, excellent

Careful: The letter *s* is silent in these words: island, aisle.

G Common Expressions

Listen and repeat these common expressions with the sound /s/.

Sorry.	**S**it **s**till.
Smile!	**S**peak **s**lowly.
Let'**s s**ee.	**S**ee you **s**oon.

UNIT 30

/z/ • zoo

-s Endings

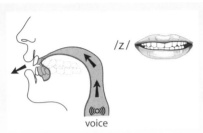

🎧 Practice the sound /s/.
Use your voice to say /z/.
Listen and repeat: /z/.

A Word Pairs

🎧 **1** Listen to these word pairs.

Sound 1: /s/	Sound 2: /z/
Sue	zoo
sip	zip
bus	buzz
price	prize
lacy	lazy

2 Listen again and repeat.

B Test Yourself

1 Listen and circle the word you hear.

1. Sue / zoo   3. bus / buzz   5. price / prize

2. C / Z   4. sip / zip   6. lacy / lazy

2 Listen to each sentence and circle the word you hear.

1. Do you spell that with a (C / Z)?

2. Do you hear a (bus / buzz)?

3. (Sip / Zip) it slowly.

4. He (races / raises) horses.

5. What's the (price / prize)?

6. She has blue (ice / eyes).

3 Practice step **2** with a partner. Say each sentence, choosing a word from the word pair. Your partner should point to the word you say.

C Vocabulary

1 Four of these words do *not* have sound /z/. Work with a partner. Circle the words that do not have the sound /z/.

buzzing	amazing	isn't	case	bees
(hissing)	these	there's	smells	says
noise	this	does	snakes	surprising

2 Listen. Repeat the words and check your answers.

D Dialog: Surprises in the post office

Zoe and Liz work at the post office. They are busy sorting packages.

1 Work with a partner. Read the dialog. Fill in the blanks with words from task C.

Zoe This box smells funny, Liz.

Liz ____There's____ something written on it.

Zoe What _____ it say?

Liz It _____: This contains six mice.

Zoe Yikes!

Liz Listen! What's in this sack?

Zoe It's making a strange _____ sound.

Sack Sssssssssssss!

    Liz Zoe! It sounds like snakes!

    Zoe Oh, it does! I wonder what's in this case, Liz.

    Liz It's making a _____ noise.

Case Zzzzzzzzzzzzz!

    Liz _____ are bees!

    Zoe A box of mice! And a sack of snakes! And a case of bees!

    Liz This is very _____.

    Zoe It's amazing. This _____ a post office, Liz. It's a zoo!

🎧 **2** Listen to the dialog and check your answers.

E   -s Endings

-s endings are used for plural nouns (*six bees*), third-person singular present tense verbs (*It smells funny*), possessives (*Zoe's house*), and contractions (*It's amazing*). All these endings follow the same pronunciation rules.

- The -s ending has three possible pronunciations: /s/, /z/, and /əz/.
- The pronunciation of the -s ending depends on the sound that comes before it in the word.

🎧 **1** Listen and repeat these plural nouns.

-s = /s/		-s = /z/		-es = /əz/	
cats	sports	dogs	animals	horses	surprises
snakes	stamps	bees	things	dishes	boxes

🎧 **2** Listen to the pronunciation of the -s endings in these verbs. Write each verb in the correct column above.

likes	owns	laughs	loses
loves	washes	collects	knows
hates	wears	watches	says

🎧 **3** Listen again. Repeat the words and check your answers to step **2**.

4 Complete these rules.

- The –*s* ending is pronounced as an extra syllable /əz/ after the sounds /s, z, ʃ, ʒ, tʃ, dʒ/.
- The –*s* ending is pronounced as the sound /____/ after other sounds made using the voice (/b, d, g, v, ð, m, n, ŋ, l, r/, and vowels).
- The –*s* ending is pronounced as the sound /____/ after other sounds made *without* using the voice (/p, t, k, f, θ/).

F Conversation Practice

1 How well do you know your classmates? Who do you think fits each sentence? Write the person's name in the blank below.

1. _____ likes dogs.
2. _____ hates snakes.
3. _____ owns two pets.
4. _____ talks to animals.
5. _____ loves surprises.
6. _____ grows flowers.

7. _____ always loses things.
8. _____ never washes dishes.
9. _____ never watches sports.
10. _____ knows a lot of jokes.
11. _____ collects stamps.
12. _____ wears contact lenses.

2 When everyone has filled in the blanks, ask questions to find out if you were right.

G Spelling

The sound /z/ is usually spelled with the letter *z* or *s*. Add more examples below.

z, zz, ze zoo, amazing, buzz, prize, _____

s easy, always, does, things, _____

se please, these, because, surprise, _____

Other spellings:

ss dessert, scissors, po<u>ss</u>ess

x pronounced /gz/: example, exactly, exist

H Common Expressions

⌒ Listen and repeat these common expressions with the sound /z/.

Please.   It wasn't easy.
Exactly!   Isn't it amazing?
Whose is it?   I was surprised.

UNIT 31

/ʃ/ • shoe
Linking Words with /ʃ/

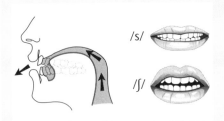

/s/

/ʃ/

🎧 Practice the sound /s/.
Put the tip of your tongue up and back a little
   to make /ʃ/.
Push your lips forward a little into a circle.
Listen and repeat: /ʃ/.

A Word Pairs

🎧 **1** Listen to these word pairs.

Sound 1: /s/		Sound 2: /ʃ/	
	Sue	shoe	
	seats	sheets	
	sell	shell	
	sign	shine	
	lease	leash	

2 Listen again and repeat.

B Test Yourself

🎧 **1** Listen to the word pairs. Write *S* if the two words are the same or *D* if the two words are different.

1. _____   2. _____   3. _____   4. _____   5. _____   6. _____

🎧 **2** Listen to each sentence and circle the word you hear.

1. Are they (Sue's / shoes)?
2. We need more (seats / sheets) for the guests.
3. Could you (sign / shine) this, please?
4. Did you (sell / shell) all the peas?
5. I can't find the (lease / leash).
6. He needs to (save / shave) more.

3 Practice step **2** with a partner. Say each sentence, choosing a word from the word pair. Your partner should point to the word you say.

C Vocabulary

🎧 **1** Listen and repeat these words with the sound /ʃ/.

shake	shrink	push	finished
sure	shouldn't	English	washing machine
short	washes	Danish	information
shirts	special	Swedish	demonstration

2 Which letters have the sound /ʃ/ in these words? Give an example of each spelling.

<u>sh (shake)</u> _____

D Dialog: A special washing machine

Shannon is shopping for a washing machine.

1 Work with a partner. Fill in the blanks with words from task C.

Shannon Do you sell washing machines?

Salesman Yes. We're having a ____<u>special</u>____ sale on this washing machine here.

Shannon Could you give me some _____ about it? Was it made in Denmark? The name looks Danish.

Salesman No, it's from Sweden. It's a _____ machine. Would you like a demonstration?

Shannon Sure. I'd like to see how it _____.

Salesman It's very simple to operate. I'll demonstrate. Here are some sheets and shirts. You put them in the machine, add soap, and shut the door. Then you just _____ this button.

Shannon The machine _____ shake like that, should it?

Salesman Washing machines always _____. (*pause*) Ah! It's _____.

Shannon But the sheets have shrunk. And look at how _____ these shirts are!

Salesman Oh, those are English sheets. English sheets always _____ a little. And those shirts were short before we washed them.

Shannon Well, I'm not _____. Could you show me another _____?

Salesman Certainly. But this is the only machine we have at the special sale price. (*pause*) We also have this dishwasher on sale. Would you like a _____?

🎧 **2** Listen to the dialog and check your answers.

E Linking Words with /ʃ/

Words in a phrase are linked together.

- /ʃ/ + /ʃ/: When /ʃ/ at the end of a word comes before /ʃ/ at the beginning of the next word, say one long /ʃ/ sound. Do not say two separate /ʃ/ sounds.
- /s/ or /z/ + /ʃ/: When the sound /s/ or /z/ comes before /ʃ/, link the two sounds and pronounce them as one long /ʃ/ sound.

🎧 **1** Listen and repeat.

English sheets	/ʃ/ + /ʃ/
this shirt	/s/ + /ʃ/
these shirts	/z/ + /ʃ/
These shirts always shrink.	/z/ + /ʃ/

2 Practice with a partner. What is another way to say the phrases below? Use an adjective to describe the nationality. Ask and answer the question.

Example: **A** What do you call ships made in Denmark?
             B Danish ships.

1. ships made in Denmark?
2. shoes made in Spain?
3. shells found in Japan?
4. shampoo from Sweden?
5. sugar from Turkey?
6. shirts from China?
7. sheep from Poland?
8. shops in Switzerland?

○ **3** Listen. Repeat the phrases and check your answers.

F Tongue Twisters

Tongue twisters are hard to say, even for native speakers. Here is a famous English tongue twister that uses the sounds /s/ and /ʃ/.

She sells seashells by the seashore.

Make up your own tongue twister using the sound /ʃ/ and practice saying it quickly.

Example: She sold six Swedish sheep.
Sheela's shop sells Irish socks.

G Spelling

The sound /ʃ/ is usually spelled *sh*, especially at the beginning or end of a word. Add more examples below.

sh show, should, finished, English, _____

In unstressed endings, the sound /ʃ/ often has one of these spellings:

ti information, demonstration, conversation, initial
ci special, especially, delicious, musician
ssi discussion, profession, Russia

Unusual spellings: <u>s</u>ure, <u>s</u>ugar, ti<u>ss</u>ue, pre<u>ss</u>ure, ma<u>ch</u>ine, <u>ch</u>ampagne, <u>Ch</u>icago, o<u>ce</u>an

H Common Expressions

○ Listen and repeat these common expressions with the sound /ʃ/.

Shhhh!   I'm going **sh**opping.
I'm not **s**ure.   What **sh**ould I do?
Are you fini**sh**ed?   I need some informa**ti**on.

/ʒ/ • television

Stress in Words with *-ion*

🎧 Practice the sound /ʃ/.
Use your voice to say /ʒ/.
Listen and repeat: /ʒ/.

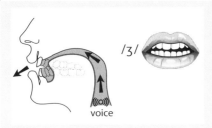

/ʒ/

A Vocabulary

🎧 **1** Listen and repeat these words with the sound /ʒ/.

measure

treasure

leisure

collision

television

Asia

casual clothes

garage

decision

Television Tonight on the Leisure Channel

6:00 PM	It's a Pleasure Special guest: the author of *Decisions, Decisions*
6:30 PM	What's the Occasion?
7:00 PM	Movie: *Treasure Island*
9:00 PM	News: An unusual collision
9:30 PM	Casual Chic
10:00 PM	Trash to Treasure
10:30 PM	Measure Twice
11:00 PM	Destination: Asia
12:00 PM	Movie: *Invasion of the Martians*

3 Work with a partner. Match the pictures with the correct television programs.

   Example: 1. *What's the Occasion?*

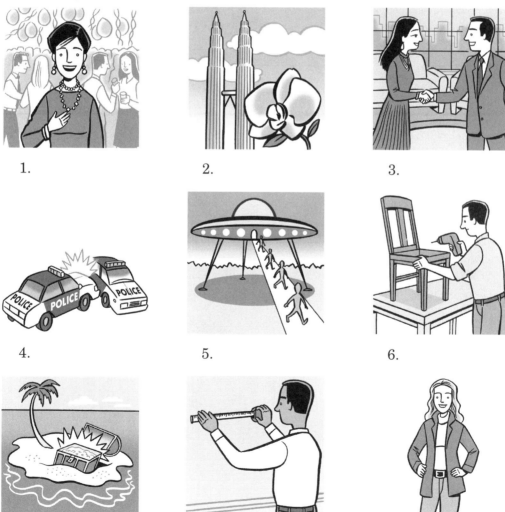

1.   2.   3.

4.   5.   6.

7.   8.   9.

B Announcement: Television tonight on the Leisure Channel

The announcer is talking about the television schedule for tonight.

🎧 Cover the TV announcement and listen. Check your answers to step **3** in task A.

Announcer Coming up next, on the Leisure Channel, the talk show *It's a Pleasure*. Tonight's special guest is the author of *Decisions, Decisions*, the book that shows you how to make the best choices.

Then stay tuned for *What's the Occasion?*, at 6:30. Planning a party? *What's the Occasion?* will show you how to make any occasion special.

At seven o'clock, be sure to watch the classic movie, *Treasure Island* – for action, adventure, and, of course, treasure!

On the nine o'clock news, find out about an unusual collision and other top news stories.

At 9:30, *Casual Chic* will feature some special clothes for casual occasions.

And at 10 o'clock, *Trash to Treasure* will show you how to make old furniture look fresh and new.

If you have trouble finding space in your garage for your car, don't miss *Measure Twice*, at 10:30. This week's project: organizing the garage.

At 11 o'clock, join *Destination: Asia* for a leisurely trip to Malaysia and Indonesia.

But don't go to sleep yet! Our midnight movie tonight is *Invasion of the Martians*.

And now here's the news . . .

C Stress in Words with *-ion*

- Words ending in *-ion* have strong stress on the syllable before the *-ion* (exception: **tel**evision).
- The sound /d/ at the end of some verbs changes to /ʒ/ when *-ion* is added to make a noun.

🎧 **1** Listen and repeat.

in**vade** – in**va**sion   ex**plode** – ex**plo**sion
de**cide** – de**ci**sion   col**lide** – col**li**sion
di**vide** – di**vi**sion

2 Fill in the blanks with an *-ion* noun related to the underlined verb.

   1. There was an unusual _____ tonight on Division Street. Two police cars collided as they chased a speeding car. The speeding car escaped.

   2. The city treasurer has decided to leave his job. He did not give a reason for his

      _____.

   3. There was an _____ in a garage on Leisure Road. A gas tank exploded when someone lit a match. Fortunately, no one was injured.

3 Listen and check your answers.

D Survey

1 The word *usually* is often pronounced as three syllables. Listen and repeat.

   usually – /**yuw** • ʒə • liy/

2 Practice in a group of three or four people. Take turns completing each sentence below. Each person should complete the sentence in a different way. Use your own phrases.

   Example: **A** I usually watch television <u>in the evening</u>.
   B I usually watch television <u>in the living room</u>.
   C I usually watch television <u>while I eat dinner</u>.

   1. I usually watch television . . .
   2. I usually use a computer . . .
   3. I usually listen to music . . .
   4. I usually read . . .
   5. I usually wear casual clothes . . .
   6. On Saturday, I usually . . .
   7. In my leisure time, I usually . . .
   8. I usually celebrate special occasions . . .

E Spelling

The sound /ʒ/ is usually spelled with the letters *s* or *ge*. Add more examples below.

   s   usually, measure, Asia, decision, _____
   ge garage, beige

Unusual spelling: seizure

F Common Expressions

Listen and repeat these common expressions with the sound /ʒ/.

Thank you. My pleasure.
What's on television?
What's your decision?

Is it a special occasion?
I usually wear casual clothes.

/tʃ/ • chips
Silent Syllables

🎧 Practice the sounds /t/ and /ʃ/.
To say /tʃ/, begin to make /t/.
Then move your tongue back and away from the
roof of your mouth as you say /ʃ/.
Do not use your voice.
Listen and repeat: /tʃ/.

1   2

A Word Pairs

🎧 **1** Listen to these word pairs.

	Sound 1: /ʃ/	**Sound 2: /tʃ/**	
	shop	chop	
	sheep	cheap	
	ships	chips	
	cash	catch	
	wash	watch	

2 Listen again and repeat.

B Test Yourself

 1 Listen and circle the word you hear.

1. sheep / cheap   3. shopping / chopping   5. cash / catch

2. ships / chips   4. wash / watch   6. shows / chose

2 Listen to each sentence and circle the word you hear.

1. I don't like (ships / chips).

2. Are those (sheep / cheap)?

3. He (shows / chose) a lot of paintings.

4. I've done all the (shopping / chopping) for dinner.

5. Could you (wash / watch) the car for me?

6. I tried to (cash / catch) the check.

3 Practice step **2** with a partner. Say each sentence, choosing a word from the word pair. Your partner should point to the word you say.

C Vocabulary

1 Listen and repeat the names of these foods.

cheese	cherries	artichokes
chicken	chocolate	spinach
chips	a chili pepper	a sandwich

2 Work with a partner. Match the pictures with the words in step **1**.

1.   2.   3.   4.   5.

6.   7.   8.   9.

D Dialog: Cooking show

Every day, Charles interviews a different chef on his cooking show, Lunch with a Chef. *Today he is interviewing Rachel Richard.*

1 Listen to the dialog. Then answer the questions.

1. Which foods in task C do Rachel and Charles talk about?

2. What is Rachel's favorite food?

3. Which food is in all three dishes she is going to make?

2 Listen again and read the dialog. Check your answers to step **1**.

Charles Hello, everyone! You're watching *Lunch with a Chef.* Today Rachel Richard, the chef at Artichoke Café, will be making lunch in our kitchen. Welcome, Rachel!

Rachel Thank you, Charles.

Charles For lunch today, Rachel will make three dishes from her restaurant, Artichoke Café. Rachel, tell us about the dishes you've chosen for the show.

Rachel Well, Charles, I'll be making spinach and artichoke dip, stuffed artichokes, and chicken with –

Charles Artichokes?

Rachel Naturally!

Charles I guess artichokes are your favorite food?

Rachel Actually, my favorite food is chocolate! But artichokes *are* my favorite vegetable.

Charles So, Rachel, which dish will you start with?

Rachel The spinach and artichoke dip.

Charles What goes into that – besides spinach and artichokes, of course? What makes your dip so rich and creamy?

Rachel Well, I use a mixture of cream cheese and cheddar cheese.

Charles Interesting. Anything else?

Rachel Yes, some chili pepper – either a fresh chili or chili powder.

Charles How much chili powder?

Rachel Oh, not too much chili powder – just a pinch.

Charles Mm, it sounds delicious! We'll be back after these commercials with two more special dishes from Artichoke Café!

E Silent Syllables

Some words have syllables that are not usually pronounced.

1 Listen. How many syllables does each word have? Write the number of syllables in the space.

1. chocølate   2   6. vegetable

2. interesting   7. favorite

3. special   8. everyone

4. temperature   9. naturally

5. delicious   10. commercials

2 Listen again. Repeat the words and check your answers. Be careful not to add any extra syllables when you say the words.

3 Which words have the sound /ʧ/?

F Discussion

Practice in a group of three to five people. Imagine that you are having guests for dinner. Plan the meal you will serve. Each dish should include a food that has the /ʃ/ or /tʃ/ sound in it.

Example: **A** First, we'll serve chips and salsa.
B For the main course, we'll have chicken with mushroom sauce, mashed potatoes, and spinach.
C Then for dessert we'll have cherry pie.

G Spelling

The sound /tʃ/ is usually spelled with the letters *ch* or *tch*. Add more examples below.

ch choose, chicken, teacher, which, _____

tch kitchen, watch, catch, match

Other spellings:

t before *u*: picture, naturally, _____

ti after *s*: question, suggestion

H Common Expressions

Listen and repeat these common expressions with the sound /tʃ/.

How mu**ch** is it?	He's an English tea**ch**er.
Cash or **ch**arge?	I'll have a **ch**eese sandwi**ch**.
Any ques**ti**ons?	Whi**ch** one did you **ch**oose?

UNIT 34

/dʒ/ • joke

Didja (*did you*); **Wouldja** (*would you*);
Didncha (*didn't you*); **Doncha** (*don't you*)

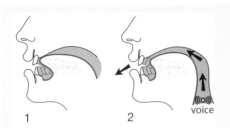

1   2   voice

🎧 Practice the sound /tʃ/.
Use your voice to say /dʒ/.
Listen and repeat: /dʒ/.

A Word Pairs

🎧 **1** Listen to these word pairs.

Sound 1: /tʃ/	Sound 2: /dʒ/
cheap	jeep
choke	joke
cheers	jeers
H	age
batch	badge

2 Listen again and repeat.

/dʒ/ • joke   **129**

B Test Yourself

🎧 **1** Listen and circle the word you hear.

    1. choke / joke   3. cheap / jeep   5. batch / badge

    2. cheer / jeer   4. cherry / Jerry   6. H's / ages

🎧 **2** Listen to each sentence and circle the word you hear.

    1. I was (choking / joking).

    2. The crowd (cheered / jeered).

    3. They didn't say their (H's / ages).

    4. Do you need another (batch / badge)?

    5. The car was (cheap / a jeep).

    6. Are those (cherries / Jerry's)?

3 Practice step **2** with a partner. Say each sentence, choosing a word from the word pair. Your partner should point to the word you say.

C Vocabulary

🎧 **1** Listen and repeat these words with the sound /ʤ/.

job	German	subjects	college	management
joking	major	psychology	knowledge	individuals
July	enjoys	graduated	change	
Japanese	agency	languages	challenge	

2 Complete the rule.

The sound /ʤ/ can be spelled with the letter *j* or with the letter _____ before *e* or the letter _____ before *u*.

D Dialog: Did you get the job?

Jess is looking for a job.

1 Work with a partner. Read the dialog. Fill in the blanks with words from task C.

    George Did you call about the job?

    Jess Which job?

    George The job managing the travel ____*agency*____ .

    Jess Oh, that job. Yes, I did.

    George What did you find out?

    Jess They want someone who graduated from _____ .

    George Well, you just _____ in June.

    Jess They're looking for someone who majored in business management.

> **Job Application**
> Name _____
> Address _____
> Education _____
> _____
> _____
> Experience _____
> _____
> _____

George Didn't you major in management before you changed your major to psychology?

Jess Actually, I didn't change majors. I had a double major – I majored in management and _____.

George If you get the _____, would you arrange travel for individuals? Or would you just do group tour packages?

Jess Oh, I'd make all kinds of travel arrangements. They want someone who's energetic and _____ challenges.

George Anyone who majors in two subjects enjoys a challenge!

Jess And they want someone with a _____ of foreign languages.

George You speak _____, don't you?

Jess Yes. And a little German.

George So, did you arrange for an interview?

Jess Yes, for _____ 6th.

George July 6th? Are you _____? That was yesterday!

Jess I'm not joking. I had the interview and I got the job!

George Hey, congratulations! Why didn't you tell me?

🎧 **2** Listen to the dialog and check your answers.

E Didja *(did you)*; Wouldja *(would you)*; Didncha *(didn't you)*; Doncha *(don't you)*

In relaxed speech, the sounds /d/ and /t/ are sometimes blended with /y/ to make a different sound.

- /d/ + /y/: The sound /d/ at the end of a word can be blended with the sound /y/ at the beginning of the next word to make the sound /ʤ/.
- /t/ + /y/: The sound /t/ at the end of a word can be blended with the sound /y/ at the beginning of the next word to make the sound /ʧ/.

🎧 **1** Listen and repeat these phrases with the sound /ʤ/.

did you   Did you call about the job?
/ʤ/   What did you find out?

would you   Would you arrange travel?
/ʤ/

🎧 **2** Listen and repeat these phrases with the sound /ʧ/.

didn't you   Why didn't you tell me?
/ʧ/   Didn't you major in management?

don't you   Don't you speak Japanese?
/ʧ/

F Scrambled Conversations

1 Practice with a partner. Student A asks a question on the left. Student B responds with a sentence from the right.

A

Why don't you tell me about yourself?
Where did you go to college?
When did you graduate?
What did you major in?
What subjects did you enjoy in school?
What would your dream job be?
What didn't you like about your last job?
Could you start on July 8th?

B

Engineering.
Yes, I could.
What would you like to know?
It wasn't challenging enough.
Managing a travel agency.
In June.
In Japan.
My favorite subjects were biology and gym.

2 Listen and check your answers.

G Role-Play

Practice in a group of two or three people. Imagine that you are at a job interview. One person wants the job. The other person or people ask questions. Use ideas from task F or your own ideas.

H Spelling

The sound /ʤ/ is usually spelled with the letter *j* or *g*. Add more examples below.

j   job, joke, enjoy, subject, _____

g   before *e, i,* or *y:* college, agency, original, psychology, _____

dge bridge, knowledge, judge

Other spelling:

d   before *u:* graduate, individual, education

I Common Expressions

Listen and repeat these common expressions with the sound /ʤ/.

I was **just** **j**oking.
When di**d** **y**ou gra**d**uate from colle**g**e?
What di**d** **y**ou ma**j**or in?

Di**d** **y**ou get the **j**ob?
Woul**d** **y**ou like some oran**g**e **j**uice?
You need a colle**g**e e**d**ucation.

Review

/s/, /z/, /ʃ/, /ʒ/, /tʃ/, and /dʒ/

A Test Yourself

🎧 Listen and circle the word you hear. You can use a dictionary if you like, but you don't have to understand every word to do this.

1. sheep / cheap / jeep
2. sack / Zack / shack
3. mass / mash / match
4. bus / buzz / budge
5. base / bays / beige
6. races / raises / rages

7. sip / zip / ship / chip
8. C / Z / she / G
9. sue / zoo / shoe / chew
10. ace / A's / H / age
11. Mars / marsh / March / Marge
12. bass / bash / batch / badge

B Vocabulary

1 Write each word in the correct column of the table below. Some words may belong in two columns.

cheese   should   wash   machines
six   gym   watch   exercise
seven   television   shopping   vegetable
lazy   sleepy   change   delicious

1: /s/	2: /z/	3: /ʃ/	4: /ʒ/	5: /tʃ/	6: /dʒ/
	cheese			cheese	

🎧 **2** Listen. Repeat the words and check your answers.

C Thoughts: Saturday decisions

It's Saturday, and Susan is thinking about what she should do.

🎧 **1** Cover the thought bubbles and listen.

2 Read the thought bubbles. Then write questions with *or* showing some of the choices you think about on Saturday or another day off. Read your questions aloud. Remember to use rising intonation on the first choice (before *or*) and falling intonation on the last choice (after *or*).

D Puzzle: Which word doesn't belong?

Circle the *-s* ending in each line that does not have the same sound as the others.

1. enjoys   wears   (watches)   sings
2. hates   likes   laughs   loses
3. Liz's   Steve's   George's   Jess's
4. dogs   horses   bees   flowers
5. jokes   boxes   glasses   dishes
6. he's   she's   it's   there's

/y/ • yes

Useta (*used to*)

/y/

🎧 Practice the sound /iy/.
To say /y/, begin to make /iy/, but *quickly*
move your tongue to make the next sound.
Do not touch the roof of your mouth
with your tongue.
Listen and repeat: /y/.

voice

A **Word Pairs**

🎧 **1** Listen to these word pairs.

Sound 1: /dʒ/	**Sound 2: /y/**
joke	yolk
jam	yam
jail	Yale
jeers	years
Jess	yes

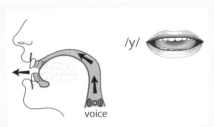

2 Listen again and repeat.

B Test Yourself

🎧 **1** Listen to the word pairs. Write *S* if the two words are the same or *D* if the two words are different.

1. _____   2. _____   3. _____   4. _____   5. _____   6. _____

🎧 **2** Listen to each sentence and circle the word you hear.

1. Their son went to (jail / Yale).
2. Did you taste the (jam / yam)?
3. I didn't get the (joke / yolk).
4. I don't like (Jell-O / yellow).
5. What (juice / use) is that?
6. (Jess / Yes), let's go.

3 Practice step **2** with a partner. Say each sentence, choosing a word from the word pair. Your partner should point to the word you say.

C Vocabulary

🎧 **1** Listen and repeat these words with the sound /y/.

young	New York	computer	familiar
yesterday	California	a few	peculiar
yoga	music	huge	university
yellow	musician	future	millionaire

2 Which letters have the sound /y/ in these words? Give an example of each spelling _y (young)_ _____ .

D Dialog: A music student

Jack and Yoko used to live in New York, but they don't live there now.

🎧 **1** Read the dialog on the next page as you listen. If you hear a word that is different from the word in your book, correct the word. Use the words in task C. There are 12 words to correct. The first one has been done for you.

Yoko Excuse me. You look ~~peculiar~~ *familiar*. Did you use to live in New York?

Jack Yes.

Yoko Did you use to work at NYU?

Jack Yes. I taught yoga there for two years.

Yoko Did you know Hugo Young? He was a yoga student.

Jack Hugo Young? Did he use to drive a huge jeep?

Yoko Yes, he did. And he used to play the piano with a jazz group at the university.

Jack Oh, yeah, I remember Hugo. A lot of people thought he was a little . . . uh . . . young. Do you know what he's doing now?

Yoko Yes. He lives in Europe, and he's a musician.

Jack A millionaire? As a jazz musician?

Yoko Oh, no. He's an executive with a familiar computer company. I just saw an interview with him on TV last year. They were asking his opinion about unusual uses for computers.

Jack Well! I guess people don't find him young anymore!

2 Listen again and check your answers.

E Useta *(used to)*

Used to (or *use to* in questions and negatives) shows that something was true in the past but is not true now.

- *Used to* and *use to* are pronounced the same.
- The words are linked together and pronounced /**yuw**stə/ ("useta").

Listen and repeat.

used to
He used to play the piano.
Did you use to live in New York?

F Conversation Practice

1 Find people in your class who fit the sentences. Walk around the classroom. Ask this question:

> When you were younger, did you use to . . . ?

2 If a person answers "yes," write the person's name in the blank. Use each person's name only once.

Example: **A** When you were younger, did you use to wear a uniform to school?
> **B** Yes, I did. / No, I didn't.

1. _____ used to wear a uniform to school.
2. _____ used to argue with his/her brothers or sisters.
3. _____ used to play the piano.
4. _____ used to do yoga.
5. _____ used to use a computer for homework.
6. _____ used to have very long hair.
7. _____ used to have an unusual job.
8. _____ used to dislike popular music.
9. _____ used to like telling jokes.

G Spelling

The sound /y/ is usually spelled with the letter *y*. The sound /y/ is also often part of the pronunciation of the spelling *u*. Add more examples below.

y you, yesterday, young, yellow, _____

u pronounced /yuw/: use, usually, university, computer, music, future, excuse, argue, huge, January

Other spellings:

i after *n* or *l*: opinion, California, familiar, million

ew, iew, eu pronounced /yuw/: few, view, interview, Europe

Unusual spelling: beautiful

H Common Expressions

Listen and repeat these common expressions with the sound /y/.

Yes, *I am.
Can I use your computer?
Do you listen to popular music?

a few years.
Where did you use to live?
the European Union

*Use the /y/ sound in /ay/ to link the two vowels here together.

/f/ • fan

Intonation in Long Sentences

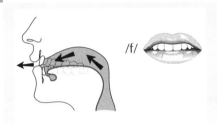

/f/

🎧 Touch your top teeth with your bottom lip.
Blow out air between your lip and teeth.
Do not use your voice.
Listen and repeat: /f/.

A Word Pairs

🎧 **1** Listen to these word pairs.

Sound 1: /p/	**Sound 2: /f/**
pan	fan
pull	full
peel	feel
copy	coffee
cup	cuff

2 Listen again and repeat.

B Test Yourself

1 Listen and circle the word you hear.

1. pan / fan	3. pull / full	5. copy / coffee
2. peel / feel	4. cup / cuff	6. past / fast

2 Listen to each sentence and circle the word you hear.

1. The sign said ("Pull" / "Full").
2. Is that an electric (pan / fan)?
3. (Peel / Feel) this orange.
4. They walked (past / fast).
5. The (copy / coffee) machine is broken.
6. Are the (cups / cuffs) clean?

3 Practice step **2** with a partner. Say each sentence, choosing a word from the word pair. Your partner should point to the word you say.

C Vocabulary

1 Listen and repeat these words with the sound /f/.

funny	front	prefer	myself
form	family	cheerful	if
first	February	photographs	laugh
phone	difficult	photographer	enough

2 Which letters have the sound /f/ in these words? Give an example of each spelling _f (funny)_ _____.

D Dialog: Family photo

Fred and Faith and their two children, Frankie and Sophie, are at a photographer's studio.

1 Work with a partner. Fill in the blanks with words from task C.

Fred I'd like a photo of _____ myself _____ and my family.

Photographer Fill out this _____, please. What size _____ would you prefer – 4×6 or 5×7?

Fred If there isn't a big difference in price, I'd _____ the 5×7.

Photographer We're offering a special this week. _____ you pay for four photos, you get the fifth one free.

Fred (*filling out the form*) Sounds fine.

Frankie Sophie stepped on my foot!

Sophie	Frankie stepped on my foot _____.
Faith	Stop fighting!
Photographer	Can the four of you sit on this sofa, please?
Sophie	I can't fit. Frankie's taking up the whole sofa!
Frankie	Am not! Your head is in _____ of my face.
Fred	That's _____! If you two don't stop fighting, we'll never get finished.
Photographer	Are you comfortable now?
	(*Frankie and Sophie frown.*)
Photographer	Mr. and Mrs. Freeman, try to laugh.
Faith	That's difficult. If you say something _____, I'll laugh.
Photographer	Frankie and Sophie, look _____ and friendly!
	(*Fred and Faith laugh.*)
Photographer	Perfect!
Fred	Will the photographs be ready by _____ first?
Photographer	Definitely. If you don't hear from us by Friday, _____ my office.

∩ **2** Listen to the dialog and check your answers.

E Intonation in Long Sentences

Long sentences often have more than one change in intonation.

- There is a short pause between main ideas.
- The intonation at the end of the first idea either rises a little ⌣͗ on the most important word or jumps up and falls a little ⌢͘ .
- At the end of the sentence, the intonation jumps up on the most important word and falls to a low note. This shows that the sentence is finished.

∩ Listen and repeat.

If you don't stop **fight**ing, we'll **nev**er get finished.

If you say something **fun**ny, I'll **laugh**.

If you don't hear from us by **Fri**day, phone my **of**fice.

F Scrambled Sentences

1 Work with a partner. Match phrases from the left column with phrases from the right column to make sentences.

If you need help,	I often laugh.
If you're finished,	you'll feel better.
If I'm free on Friday,	don't forget to buy fish.
If I have enough money,	ask your father.
If I drink coffee after dinner,	you can't watch TV.
If I feel nervous,	I'll go to my friend's party.
If you forget the phone number,	feel free to leave.
If you go shopping for food,	I can't fall asleep.
If you get some fresh air,	I'll go to France.
If you don't finish your homework,	call 555-1212.

2 Listen and check your answers.

3 Choose three phrases from the left column. Use your own words to complete the three sentences.

G Spelling

The sound /f/ is usually spelled with the letter *f*. Add more examples below.

f   first, funny, before, _____

ff   off, office, difficult, _____

Other spellings:

ph telephone, photograph, alphabet
gh laugh, enough, cough

H Common Expressions

Listen and repeat these common expressions with the sound /f/.

Don't **f**orget.
Have **f**un!
How do you **f**eel? I **f**eel **f**ine.

Is it **f**ar **f**rom here?
It's **f**ive a**f**ter **f**our.
Fill out this **f**orm.

UNIT 38

/v/ • very

Weak and Strong Pronunciations of *have*

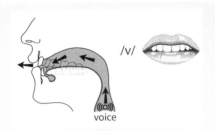

/v/

🎧 Practice the sound /f/.
Use your voice to say /v/.
Listen and repeat: /v/.

voice

A Word Pairs 1

🎧 **1** Listen to these word pairs.

Sound 1: /b/	Sound 2: /v/
ban	van
B	V
best	vest
boat	vote
cabs	calves

2 Listen again and repeat.

🎧 **1** Listen to these word pairs.

	Sound 1: /f/	**Sound 2: /v/**	
	fan	van	
	fine	vine	
	few	view	
	leaf	leave	

2 Listen again and repeat.

C Test Yourself

🎧 **1** Listen and circle the word you hear.

1. boat / vote   3. fine / vine   5. belief / believe

2. cabs / calves   4. leaf / leave   6. ban / fan / van

🎧 **2** Listen to each sentence and circle the word you hear.

1. One person – one (boat / vote).

2. I want to get the (best / vest).

3. This room has a (few / view).

4. Do you want (a leaf / to leave)?

5. We use our (fan / van) in the summer.

6. We saw two (cabs / calves) on the road.

3 Practice step **2** with a partner. Say each sentence, choosing a word from the word pair. Your partner should point to the word you say.

D Vocabulary

🎧 **1** Listen and repeat these words with the sound /v/.

very	visit	river	five
valley	November	living	moved
view	favorite	love	traveled

2 Describe the picture. Use as many words as possible with the sound /v/.

E Dialog: A view of the valley

Vivian is visiting Victor at his house in the mountains.

1 Work with a partner. Read the dialog and circle the correct words in parentheses.

Vivian How long (did you live / have you lived) here?

Victor Five and a half years. (We moved / We've moved) here on November first.

Vivian You have a fantastic view.

Victor Thanks. Look, Vivian, you can see the river down in the valley.

Vivian It's a beautiful view. (I traveled / I've traveled) all over, and this is one of my very favorite places.

Victor Yes, (I love / I've loved) living here.

Vivian And (I love / I've loved) visiting!

🎧 **2** Listen to the dialog and check your answers.

F Weak and Strong Pronunciations of *have*

The word *have* usually has a weak pronunciation when it is used with another verb: *How long have you lived here?*

- Link the weak pronunciation of *have* to the word before it.
- *Have* is usually contracted after a pronoun (*I've, you've,* etc.).

When *have* is used without another verb, it has a stronger pronunciation.

🎧 **1** Listen and repeat the weak pronunciation. The word *have* sounds like *of* in this question.

/əv/
How long have you lived here?

🎧 **2** Listen and repeat the contracted form.

/v/
I've lived here for five years.

🎧 **3** Listen and repeat. The word *have* has a stronger pronunciation in these two sentences.

/hæv/
You have a fantastic view.

/hæv/
Yes, I have.

G Conversation Practice

1 Practice with a partner. Use the words below to make questions with *have*. Then take turns asking and answering the questions.

Example: **A** How long have you lived here?
　　　　　 B I've lived here for a year and a half.

1. How long . . . lived here?
2. . . . a house or an apartment?
3. . . . a good view from your house?
4. . . . lived in a lot of places?
5. . . . traveled a lot?
6. How many countries . . . visited?

2 Work with your partner to write a conversation. Use ideas from the dialog on page 145 or your own ideas.

3 Practice your conversation.

H Spelling

The sound /v/ is usually spelled with the letter *v*. Add more examples below.

v   very, visit, river, have, love, _____

Unusual spelling: o<u>f</u>

Careful: Words ending with the sound /v/ always add the letter *e* in the spelling. English words do not end in the letter *v*.

I Common Expressions

🎧 Listen and repeat these common expressions with the sound /v/.

I don't believe it.
It's very expensive.
How long have you lived here?

I've lived here for five years.
Have you ever been there?
I've never been there.

/w/ • wet

Wh- Questions with Rising Intonation

Practice the sound /uw/.
Make your lips round and hard for /w/.
Quickly relax your lips.
Listen and repeat: /w/.

/w/

A Word Pairs

1 Listen to these word pairs.

Sound 1: /v/	Sound 2: /w/
v	we
vet	wet
vest	west
vine	wine
veil	whale

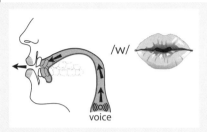

2 Listen again and repeat.

B Test Yourself

🎧 **1** Listen to the word pairs. Write *S* if the two words are the same or *D* if the two words are different.

1. _____ 2. _____ 3. _____ 4. _____ 5. _____ 6. _____

🎧 **2** Listen to each sentence and circle the word you hear.

1. Does this say ("V" / "we")?

2. Look for it in the (vest / west).

3. What kind of (vine / wine) is this?

4. The (veils / whales) were gray.

5. The other book was (verse / worse).

6. I think she's (a vet / wet).

3 Practice step **2** with a partner. Say each sentence, choosing a word from the word pair. Your partner should point to the word you say.

C Vocabulary

🎧 **1** Listen. How many /w/ sounds do you hear in each phrase?

_2_ a heavy wool sweater	_____ around one
_____ very windy	_____ saw him on Wednesday
_____ went for a walk	_____ twelve
_____ near the highway	_____ it was very quiet
_____ the whole day	_____ walking in the woods
_____ watched the squirrels	_____ we walked quickly

2 Listen again. Repeat the phrases and check your answers.

D Dialog: A walk in the woods

Wendy went for a walk with William. She is telling her friend Valerie about it.

1 Work with a partner. Read the dialog on pages 149 and 150. Fill in the blanks with phrases from task C.

Valerie What's happening with William? Did you see him this week?

Wendy Yeah. I <u>saw him on Wednesday</u>. We went for a walk.

Valerie What did you do?

Wendy I said we _____.

Valerie Where did you walk?

Wendy In the woods.

Valerie Where?

Wendy In the woods. You know, the woods _____.

Valerie Wasn't it cold and wet on Wednesday?

Wendy Well, it was cold and _____, but not wet. I wore _____, and _____ to keep warm.

Valerie I love _____. It's so peaceful and quiet.

Wendy Yeah, _____ once we got away from the highway. There were birds and squirrels everywhere.

Valerie Wow, it sounds wonderful. Did you spend _____ in the woods?

Wendy No. William had to work in the afternoon. I went home _____.

Valerie What did you do for lunch?

Wendy We brought sandwiches with us. We stopped for lunch around _____, and we sat and _____ for a while, but it was too windy to sit long.

Valerie Well, it sounds like a very nice walk, anyway.

Wendy It was.

∩ **2** Listen to the dialog and check your answers.

E *Wh-* Questions with Rising Intonation

Wh- questions (questions with *Who? What? Where? When? Why? How?*) usually end with falling intonation, but they can also end with rising intonation.

- Use a *Wh-* question with falling intonation (⌒) to ask for new information. In falling intonation, the voice jumps up on the most important word and then goes down at the end.
- You can use a *Wh-* question with rising intonation (⌣) if you aren't sure what someone said and you want the person to repeat it. In rising intonation, the voice goes up at the end.

∩ **1** Listen. Speaker B is asking for new information.

    A Wendy saw William this week.

    B When did she **see** him?

    A On Wednesday.

∩ **2** Listen. Speaker B is asking A to repeat.

    A Wendy saw William this week.

    B **When** did she see him?

    A This week.

F Conversation Practice

1 Work with a partner. Read the conversation below. Draw an arrow after each of Speaker B's *Wh-* questions to show whether it should have rising intonation (↗) or falling (↘) intonation.

A I'm going to a wedding
this weekend.
B What? ↗
A I'm going to a wedding.
B Who's getting married? ____
A Willa.
B Who? ____
A Willa – a woman I work with.
B When did you say the wedding was? ____
A This weekend.
B When? ____
A Sunday at twelve.
B What are you going to wear? ____
A A black-and-white wool suit.

2 Listen to the conversation and check your answers. Then practice the conversation with your partner.

G Spelling

The sound /w/ is usually spelled with the letter *w*. Add more examples below.

w walk, woods, wear, would, _____

Other spellings:

wh what, when, while, everywhere, _____

u after the letter *q* and sometimes after the letter *g* or *s*: quiet, question, squirrel, language, persuade

o one, once, everyone

Careful: The letter *w* is silent in these words: write, wrong, wrist, answer, two, who, whole.

H Common Expressions

Listen and repeat these common expressions with the sound /w/.

You're **w**elcome.	**Wh**ere do you **w**ork?
Don't **w**orry.	**Wh**at lang**u**ages do you speak?
What **w**ould you like?	The class meets **o**nce a **w**eek.

UNIT 40
/h/ • how

Dropped /h/; Intonation in Exclamations

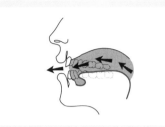

🎧 Open your mouth.
Quickly push out a lot of air.
Do not use your voice.
Do not touch the roof of your mouth with
    your tongue.
Listen and repeat: /h/.

A Word Pairs

🎧 **1** Listen to these word pairs.

Sound 1: (no /h/)	**Sound 2: /h/**
eat	heat
old	hold
eye	high
air	hair
earring	hearing

2 Listen again and repeat.

B Test Yourself

🎧 **1** Listen and circle the word you hear.

   1. I / high   3. eat / heat   5. ate / hate

   2. old / hold   4. air / hair   6. art / heart

🎧 **2** Listen to each sentence and circle the word you hear.

   1. It was (I / high).

   2. What nice clean (air / hair)!

   3. Did you (eat / heat) the soup?

   4. What did they say about his (art / heart)?

   5. I (ate / hate) eggs for breakfast.

   6. There's something wrong with my (earring / hearing).

3 Practice step **2** with a partner. Say each sentence, choosing a word from the word pair. Your partner should point to the word you say.

C Vocabulary

1 In one of the words in each column, the letter *h* is usually silent. Work with a partner. Make an X through the silent *h*'s.

how	house	vehicle	hope	home
who	hours	hit	horrible	what
o̶h̶	hurt	behind	happened	hospital
heard	husband	half	exhausted	unharmed

🎧 **2** Listen. Repeat the words and check your answers.

D Dialog: A horrible accident

Ellen is telling Helen about a car accident.

1 Work with a partner. Read the dialog on pages 153 and 154. Fill in the blanks with words from task C.

Helen Hi, Ellen.

 Ellen Oh, Helen, have you ___heard___ about Henry?

Helen Who?

 Ellen Henry Harris – Hannah's _____. He was in a car accident.

Helen Oh, no! What _____?

 Ellen He had an accident on his way _____ from work.

Helen How awful! Was he _____?

 Ellen Yeah. He was taken to the hospital in an ambulance.

Helen That's horrible! _____ did it happen?

Ellen A vehicle _____ him from behind. It happened about _____
a mile from his house.

Helen How horrible! Is he still in the _____?

Ellen Yeah. He's having an operation tomorrow. Poor Hannah! She's _____.
She's been at the hospital for _____.

Helen Was the other driver hurt, too?

Ellen No, he was completely _____.

Helen I _____ Henry will be all right.

Ellen I hope so, too.

∩ **2** Listen to the dialog and check your answers.

E Dropped /h/

Pronouns like *he, his, him,* and *her* are usually unstressed and have a weak pronunciation.

- The sound /h/ in these pronouns is often dropped (not pronounced) when the pronoun is in the middle or at the end of a sentence.
- If you drop the /h/, link the rest of the pronoun to the word before it.
- The sound /h/ is pronounced when the pronoun comes at the beginning of a sentence or after a pause.

∩ **1** Listen and repeat. The sound /h/ is dropped in these examples.

was he (sounds like "wuzzy")   Was he hurt?

hit him   A vehicle hit him from behind.

∩ **2** Listen and repeat. The sound /h/ is pronounced in these examples.

He was in a car accident.   No, he was completely unharmed.

F Intonation in Exclamations

To show strong feeling:

- the voice goes up very high before it falls
- the important words are extra long.

∩ Listen and repeat.

Oh, **no**!   How **hor**rible!   How ex**ci**ting!

How **aw**ful!   How **won**derful!   That's **hor**rible!

G Conversation Practice

🎧 **1** Practice with a partner. Student A uses the names and sentences in the table, in any order. Student B responds with an exclamation from task F. Listen to this example.

> **A** Have you heard about Harry?
> **B** No. What happened?
> **A** He spent his whole vacation in the hospital.
> **B** How awful!

NAMES	SENTENCES
Harry	He had an accident and had to go to the hospital.
Henry	He had a heart attack.
Hannah	He won eight hundred dollars.
Anna	He hurt both his hands and can't hold anything.
Hannah's father	She and her husband bought a huge house in Hawaii.
Anna's husband	She fell off a horse and hit her head.
Howard	A helicopter hit his house.
Andrew	He spent his whole vacation in the hospital.

2 Look at the sentences in the table. Where could you drop the sound /h/?

H Spelling

The sound /h/ is usually spelled with the letter *h*. Add more examples below.

> **h**   how, hope, heart, unhappy, _____

Other spelling:

> **wh**   who, whose, whole

Careful: The letter *h* is silent in these words: h̸our, h̸onest, h̸onor, h̸eir, oh̸, veh̸icle, exh̸austed, exh̸ibit, rh̸yme, rh̸ythm.

I Common Expressions

🎧 Listen and repeat these common expressions with the sound /h/.

Hi! How are you?	I **hope** so.
Happy Holidays!	What **happened?**
Can I **help** you?	**Have** you **heard?**

/θ/ • think

Using Stress and Intonation to Show Surprise

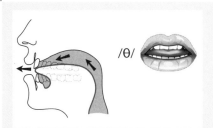

/θ/

🎧 Put the tip of your tongue between your
front teeth.
Blow out air between your tongue and
top teeth.
Do not use your voice.
Listen and repeat: /θ/.

A Word Pairs 1

🎧 **1** Listen to these word pairs.

	Sound 1: /s/	**Sound 2:** /θ/	
	sick	thick	
	sum	thumb	
	sink	think	
	mouse	mouth	
	pass	path	

2 Listen again and repeat.

B Word Pairs 2

🎧 **1** Listen to these word pairs.

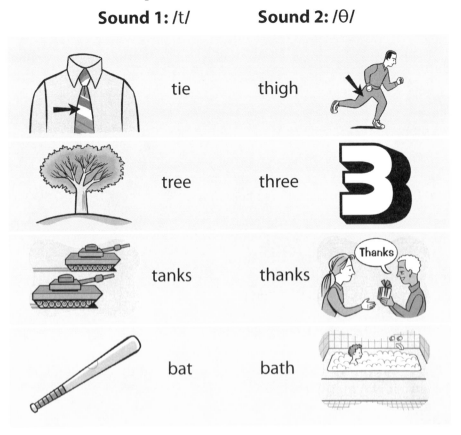

	Sound 1: /t/	**Sound 2:** /θ/	
	tie	thigh	
	tree	three	
	tanks	thanks	
	bat	bath	

2 Listen again and repeat.

C Test Yourself

🎧 **1** Listen and circle the word you hear.

1. sink / think   3. tree / three   5. sick / tick / thick

2. mouse / mouth   4. bat / bath   6. sank / tank / thank

🎧 **2** Listen to each sentence and circle the word you hear.

1. I hope they're not too (sick / thick).

2. Send (tanks / thanks).

3. She (taught / thought) for a long time.

4. I always (sink / think) in the pool.

5. It's not (true / through), is it?

6. The (bat / bath) was very small.

3 Practice step **2** with a partner. Say each sentence, choosing a word from the word pair. Your partner should point to the word you say.

D Vocabulary

🎧 Listen and repeat these words with the sound /θ/.

thank you	thirsty	author	birthday	fourth
thought	Thursday	anything	athlete	worth
thousand	thirty-three	something	math	month

E Dialog: Gossip

Ethan is surprised at some things Beth tells him.

🎧 **1** Listen to the dialog. One important word stands out in each sentence. Underline the word that stands out in each numbered sentence. The other sentences have been done for you.

Beth Kathy Roth is thirty-<u>three</u>.
Ethan <u>Is</u> she?   1. I thought she was forty-three.
Beth Her birthday was last <u>Thursday</u>.
Ethan <u>Was</u> it?   2. I thought it was last month.
Beth Seth is her third <u>husband</u>.
Ethan <u>Is</u> he?   3. I thought he was her fourth husband.
Beth Their house is worth three hundred thousand <u>dollars</u>.
Ethan <u>Is</u> it?   4. I thought it was worth about one hundred thousand dollars.
Beth Seth is the author of a <u>math</u> book.
Ethan <u>Is</u> he?   5. I thought he was an athlete.
Beth I'm so <u>thirsty</u>.
Ethan <u>Are</u> you? I thought you had something to drink at <u>Kathy's</u> house.
Beth No. Kathy didn't <u>offer</u> me anything.
Ethan <u>I'll</u> buy you a drink.
Beth <u>Oh</u>! <u>Thank</u> you.

2 Listen again and check your answers.

F Using Stress and Intonation to Show Surprise

To show surprise, you can ask a short question with rising intonation.

🎧 **1** Listen to these short questions.

A Kathy Roth is thirty-three.   **A** Her birthday was last Thursday.

B Is she?   **B Was** it?

To show a contrast, put strong stress on the information that is different.

- The stressed syllable of this word sounds **loud** and s l o w.
- The intonation changes on this word. In a sentence with falling intonation, the voice jumps up on the stressed syllable and then falls.

2 Listen and repeat.

A Kathy Roth is thirty-**three**.

B Is she? I thought she

was **for**ty-three.

A Her birthday was last **Thurs**day.

B Was it? I thought it was

last **month**.

G Conversation Practice

Work with a partner. Correct the mistakes in the sentences. Student A says the incorrect sentence. Student B shows surprise and then corrects the mistake. Listen to this example.

A March is the fourth month of the year.
B Is it? I thought it was the third month of the year.

1. August is the seventh month of the year.
2. New York is south of Miami.
3. There are four feet in a yard.
4. Athens is north of Rome.
5. Agatha Christie was a famous author of history books.
6. Valentine's Day is on January 14th.
7. New Year's Eve is on December 30th.
8. Last year was 2005.

H Spelling

The sound /θ/ is spelled with the letters *th*. Add more examples below.

th think, thousand, something, month, _____

I Common Expressions

Listen and repeat these common expressions with the sound /θ/.

Thank you.
I **th**ink so.
Thanks for **th**inking of me!

I'm **th**irsty.
Today is my **th**ir**th** bir**th**day.
I'm free on Tuesdays and **Th**ursdays.

/ð/ • the other

Weak Pronunciations for *the* and *than*

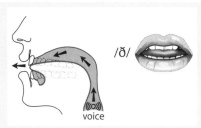

🎧 Practice the sound /θ/.
Use your voice to say /ð/.
Listen and repeat: /ð/.

A Word Pairs 1

🎧 **1** Listen to these word pairs.

	Sound 1: /d/	**Sound 2:** /ð/	
	day	they	
	dare	there	
	doze	those	
	ladder	lather	
	breed	breathe	

2 Listen again and repeat.

B Word Pairs 2

🎧 **1** Listen to these word pairs.

Sound 1: /z/	**Sound 2: /ð/**
closing	clothing
bays	bathe
breeze	breathe
tease	teethe

🎧 **2** Listen again and repeat.

C Test Yourself

🎧 **1** Listen and circle the word you hear.

1. day / they
2. letter / leather
3. tease / teethe
4. closing / clothing
5. D's / Z's / these
6. breed / breeze / breathe

🎧 **2** Listen to each sentence and circle the word you hear.

1. The sign said ("Closing" / "Clothing").
2. We waited until (day / they) came.
3. The child was just (teasing / teething).
4. Try to pronounce (D's / Z's / these) more clearly.
5. They're (breeding / breathing) like rabbits.
6. Did you see the (letter / leather)?

3 Practice step **2** with a partner. Say each sentence, choosing a word from the word pair. Your partner should point to the word you say.

D Vocabulary

1 One word in each column has the sound /θ/ and not /ð/. Work with a partner. Circle the words that have the sound /θ/.

this	there	weather	Thursday
that	three	another	rather
(think)	together	anything	smoother
though	leather	either	the other

🎧 **2** Listen. Repeat the words and check your answers.

E Dialog: The jacket in the window

Heather is shopping for a new jacket.

1 Work with a partner. Read the dialog. Fill in the blanks with words from task D. You can use a word more than once.

Heather I'd like to buy that jacket in the window.

Salesclerk Well, ____there____ are three jackets _____ in the window. Do you want the one with the feather collar?

Heather No. The other one. The leather one.

Salesclerk The one with the zipper?

Heather No, not _____ one either. That one over _____. The one that's on sale.

Salesclerk Oh, that one. Now, here's _____ leather jacket that I think you'd like.

Heather But this one is more expensive than the one in the window.

Salesclerk It's a better jacket than the other one. The _____ is smoother.

Heather I'd _____ get the one in the window, though. I think that one is better for cold _____.

Salesclerk Well, fine, if _____'s the one you want. But we don't take _____ out of the window until three o'clock on Thursday.

🎧 **2** Listen to the dialog and check your answers.

F Weak Pronunciations for *the* and *than*

The words *the* and *than* are normally unstressed and have weak pronunciations.

- Before a consonant sound, *the* is pronounced /ðə/, with the short, unstressed vowel /ə/.
- Before a vowel sound, *the* is often pronounced /ðiy/. The /iy/ sound is short. Use the /y/ sound in /iy/ to link *the* to the following vowel.
- *Than* is pronounced /ðən/, with the short unstressed vowel /ə/.

🎧 Listen and repeat.

/ðə/   /ðə/
the **one*** with the **zip**per

/ðiy/
the others

       /ðən/
better than the **oth**ers

Which jacket do you **think** is **bet**ter than the **oth**ers?

I **think** the **one** with the **belt** is **bet**ter than the **oth**ers.

*The word *one* begins with a consonant sound /w/, even though it begins with a vowel letter o.

G Conversation Practice

Work with a partner. Talk about the four jackets using words from the list below.

A Which jacket do you think is _____ than the others?

| **B** I think the | one with the belt
leather jacket
one with the zipper
jacket for $130 | is
looks | _____ than the others. |

better	more at**trac**tive	more **styl**ish
warmer	more **com**fortable	more **prac**tical
dressier	more ex**pen**sive	more **cas**ual

H Spelling

The sound /ð/ is spelled with the letters *th*. Add more examples below.

    th   there, that, another, together, _____

Careful: The *th* in *clothes* is usually silent.

I Common Expressions

Listen and repeat these common expressions with the sound /ð/.

my mo**th**er and fa**th**er	ei**th**er **th**is one or **th**at one
What's **th**e wea**th**er like?	Did **th**ey go **th**ere toge**th**er?
I'd ra**th**er not answer **th**at.	**Th**is one is better **th**an **th**e others.

Review
/y/, /f/, /v/, /w/, /h/, /θ/, and /ð/

A Test Yourself

🎧 Listen and circle the word you hear. You can use a dictionary if you like, but you don't have to understand every word to do this.

1. best / vest / west   7. tree / free / three
2. berry / ferry / very   8. den / Zen / then
3. fine / vine / wine   9. leap / leaf / leave
4. pool / fool / who'll   10. tense / tent / tenth
5. you / few / hue   11. breed / breeze / breathe
6. ear / year / hear   12. tease / teeth / teethe

B Conversations

🎧 **1** Listen to B's response in each conversation below and underline the word that stands out the most. Then put a check √ next to the sentence that A probably said.

1. **A** _____ Do you work in New York?

       _√_ Did you use to live in New York?

    B No, but I used to <u>work</u> there.

2. **A** _____ Does he have any brothers or sisters?

       _____ I think he has three brothers.

    B He has four brothers.

3. **A** _____ How long have they lived here?

       _____ They've lived here for five years.

    B More than five years.

4. **A** _____ When is her interview?

       _____ Her interview is at 1:30.

    B I think it's at 12:30.

5. **A** _____ Does he have any brothers or sisters?

       _____ I think he has three brothers.

    B He has four brothers.

6. **A** _____ When is her interview?

       _____ Her interview is at 1:30.

    B I think it's at 12:30.

7. **A** ____ Do you work in New York?

____ Did you use to live in New York?

B No, but I used to work there.

8. **A** ____ How long have they lived here?

____ They've lived here for five years.

B More than five years.

2 Listen and check your answers.

3 Practice the conversations with a partner. For each conversation, one person says one of A's sentences. The other person gives B's response, making the correct word stand out.

C Puzzle: Which word doesn't belong?

Circle the word in each line that does not have the same consonant sound underlined in the first word.

1. thanks	there	anything	months	three
2. very	of	view	live	often
3. funny	laughed	phone	thought	first
4. how	who	why	hope	whole
5. went	question	one	only	when
6. that	other	clothing	nothing	rather
7. yes	computer	few	quickly	million

UNIT 44 /m/ • me

Using Intonation to Change Meaning

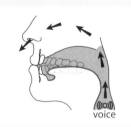

🎧 Close your lips.
Use your voice.
The sound /m/ comes through your nose.
Listen and repeat: /m/.

voice

A Vocabulary

🎧 Listen and repeat these words with the sound /m/.

make	summer	time
met	small	comes
remember	smart	Mom
tomorrow	home	homemade

B Dialog: Mom's muffins

Sam is talking to his mother. He invited a friend from school to come to his house for lunch.

1 Work with a partner. Read the dialog. Fill in the blanks with words from task A.

Sam Mom?

Mom Mm?

Sam Can my friend Tom come _____home_____ with me for lunch tomorrow?

Mom Mm, I guess so. Have I _____ Tom before?

Sam Mm-hm. You met him in the _____. He's small and really _____ in math.

Mom Mm, I _____ Tom. His family _____ from Maine, right?

Sam Mm-hm, that's him. Oh, um, Mom? Can you _____ some _____ muffins tomorrow?

Mom Mm . . . maybe. If I have _____.

Sam But _____, I told Tom about your muffins. That's why he's coming for lunch _____!

🎧 **2** Listen to the dialog and check your answers.

C Using Intonation to Change Meaning

Mm can have many meanings. The meaning changes when you change the intonation.

🎧 Listen.

Mm means "What did you say?"   Mm means "I'm thinking."

Mm means "Yes."   Mm means "This is good!" or "This is delicious!"

D Conversation

🎧 **1** Listen to this conversation. Say which meaning *Mm* has in B's answers.

A Would you like some homemade muffins?   **B** Mm?

A Would you like some muffins?   **B** Mm.

A Here you go.   **B** (*eating*) Mm!

A I'm glad you like them. I made them myself.
Would you like jam with them?   **B** Mm?

A Jam.   **B** Mm . . .

A They're yummy with jam. Want some?   **B** Mm.

A Here you are.   **B** (*eating*) Mm!

2 Practice the conversation with a partner.

E Spelling

The sound /m/ is spelled with the letter *m*. Add more examples below.

m   maybe, family, home, I'm, _____

mm   summer, swimming, yummy

Other spellings:

mb   *b* is silent: comb, lamb, climb

mn   *n* is silent: autumn, column

F Common Expressions

🎧 Listen and repeat these common expressions with the sound /m/.

My name is . . .   Have so**me** **m**ore.

I'**m** sorry.   So**me**ti**m**es.

I don't re**mem**ber.   **M**aybe.

/n/ • no
Syllabic /n/

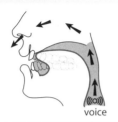
voice

🎧 Put the tip of your tongue on the roof of your mouth just behind your top teeth.
Do not close your lips.
Use your voice.
The sound /n/ comes through your nose.
Listen and repeat: /n/.

A Word Pairs

🎧 **1** Listen to these word pairs.

Sound 1: /m/		**Sound 2: /n/**	
	me	knee	
	mail	nail	
	mine	nine	
	comb	cone	
	gum	gun	

2 Listen again and repeat.

B Test Yourself

🎧 **1** Listen and circle the word you hear.

1. mail / nail	3. mine / nine	5. gum / gun
2. me / knee	4. comb / cone	6. M / N

🎧 **2** Listen to each sentence and circle the word you hear.

1. Can you pick up the (mail / nail)?
2. I'd like two (combs / cones), please.
3. I'll give you (mine / nine).
4. Be careful – don't step on the (gum / gun)!
5. Isn't the homework (dumb / done)?
6. Do you spell that with one (M / N) or two?

3 Practice step **2** with a partner. Say each sentence, choosing a word from the word pair. Your partner should point to the word you say.

C Vocabulary

🎧 **1** Listen and repeat these words with the sound /n/.

new	neighborhood	don't
nice	midnight	tenant
noise	spend	convenient

🎧 **2** Say /n/ clearly at the end of a word. Listen and repeat.

one	seven	kitchen
nine	eleven	downtown
fifteen	I mean	train station

🎧 **3** Link /n/ at the end of a word to a following vowel. Listen and repeat.

an apartment   an oven   on a bus line

D Dialog: At a rental agency

Martin is looking for an apartment to rent. He is talking to a rental agent.

🎧 **1** Read the dialog as you listen. Circle the words you hear. Do you hear two separate words or a contraction?

°For Rent°
One-bedroom
apartment

Martin Good morning. (I am / I'm) interested in renting a one-bedroom apartment downtown.

Agent Certainly. (We have / We've) a nice apartment on the corner of Main Street and Central Avenue. (It has / It's) big windows, a new kitchen, and a very convenient location. And (it is / it's) only $1,120 a month.

Martin I (could not / couldn't) pay $1,120 a month. (I am / I'm) a student.

Agent A student, hmm. . . . How much can you spend?

Martin Well, I (did not / didn't) want to spend more than $700 a month.

Agent $700 a month? We (do not / don't) often have apartments as inexpensive as that. Not in the center of town, anyway. (We have / We've) got one apartment for $790 a month.

Martin (Where is / Where's) it? Is it in the same neighborhood?

Agent No, it (is not / isn't). (It is / It's) on Seventh Avenue, near the train station.

Martin I (do not / don't) know. I mean, I need to be near the university.

Agent (It is / It's) on a bus line. (It has / It's) a kitchen, but the kitchen (does not / doesn't) have an oven.

Martin No oven? Well, a nice kitchen (is not / isn't) that important to me.

Agent (There is / There's) a garden in the front, but the tenants (cannot / can't) use it. The landlord lives downstairs. Friends are forbidden in the apartment after midnight. No noise and no television after 11:15. No –

Martin No, thank you! I want an apartment, not a prison!

2 Listen again and check your answers.

E Syllabic /n/

Sometimes the sound /n/ makes a syllable without any vowel sound. This is called "syllabic /n/."

- Syllabic /n/ occurs only in unstressed syllables.
- Syllabic /n/ usually comes after another consonant made with the tip of the tongue just behind your top teeth: /t/, /d/, /s/, or /z/.

1 Listen and repeat. Try not to move the tip of your tongue between the sound /d/, /z/, or /t/ and the following /n/.

garden	**isn**'t	**writ**ten
for**bid**den	**doesn**'t	**got**ten
student	**did**n't	im**por**tant
prison	**could**n't	**cer**tainly

2 Listen and repeat. The word *and* is often pronounced as a syllabic /n/.

790   "seven hundred 'n' ninety"

1,120   "eleven hundred 'n' twenty" or "one thousand one hundred 'n' twenty"

Main Street and ('n') Central Avenue

no noise and ('n') no television

F Conversation Practice

Work with a partner. Take turns asking and answering questions about the dialog. Use short answers like "No, he didn't" / "No, he isn't" / "Yes, he is."

1. Is Martin looking for a house in the country?
2. Does he want an apartment with two bedrooms?
3. Is Martin a student?
4. Did he want to spend $1,120 a month?
5. Does the second apartment have a kitchen?
6. Does the kitchen have an oven?
7. Could Martin make noise after midnight?
8. Did Martin rent the apartment?

G Discussion

Practice in a group of three or four people. Talk about the things that are important to you in renting an apartment. Which things below are most important to you? Which things are not important?

no noise	a new kitchen	near transportation
convenient location	a nice neighborhood	friends nearby
low rent	a nice landlord	a garden

H Spelling

The sound /n/ is usually spelled with the letter *n*. Add more examples below.

n   new, name, downtown, none, _____

nn funny, dinner, beginning

Other spellings:

kn *k* is silent: know, knee, knife, knock
gn *g* is silent: foreign, sign, design

Careful: The letter *n* is silent in these words: column, autumn.

I Common Expressions

🎧 Listen and repeat these common expressions with the sound /n/.

No, I did**n**'t.	I'll be ready **in** a mi**n**ute.
I do**n**'t want to.	I don't **kn**ow the a**n**swer.
Not **n**ow.	I'm **n**ot do**n**e.

UNIT 46 /ŋ/ • sing

Weak Pronunciation and Contraction of *be*

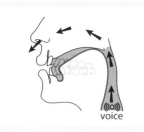

🎧 Touch the back of the roof of your mouth with
  the back of your tongue.
Use your voice.
The sound /ŋ/ comes through your nose.
Listen and repeat: /ŋ/.

A Word Pairs 1

🎧 **1** Listen to these word pairs.

Sound 1: /n/		Sound 2: /ŋ/	
	thin	thing	
	ban	bang	
	ran	rang	
	fans	fangs	
	wins	wings	

2 Listen again and repeat.

B Word Pairs 2

🎧 **1** Listen to these word pairs.

Sound 1: /ŋk/   **Sound 2:** /ŋ/

think	thing	
bank	bang	
sink	sing	
rink	ring	

2 Listen again and repeat.

C Test Yourself

🎧 **1** Listen to the word pairs. Write *S* if the two words are the same or *D* if the two words are different.

1. _____   2. _____   3. _____   4. _____   5. _____   6. _____

🎧 **2** Listen to each sentence and circle the word you hear.

1. Don't let him (sink / sing)!
2. They (banned / banged) the books.
3. Watch out for those (fans / fangs).
4. I want (to win / a wing).
5. The (rink / ring) was a perfect circle.
6. They should (ban / bank / bang) it.

3 Practice step **2** with a partner. Say each sentence, choosing a word from the word pair. Your partner should point to the word you say.

D Vocabulary

🎧 Listen and repeat these words with the sound /ŋ/.

string	falling	sleeping	standing
pink	running	yelling	helping
morning	talking	tying	reaching

E Dialog: Noisy neighbors

Frank is trying to sleep. Ingrid is looking out the window at their neighbors, the Kings.

🎧 **1** Read the dialog as you listen. If you hear a word that is different from the word in your book, correct the word. Use the words in task D. There are 12 words to correct. The first one has been done for you.

Frank (*angrily*) Bang! Bang! Bang! What are the Kings doing? It's seven o'clock on Sunday ~~evening~~ morning, and we're trying to sleep!

Ingrid They're singing very loudly.

Frank Yes, but what's the banging noise, Ingrid?

Ingrid (*looking out the window*) Ron is sitting on a ladder and banging some nails into the wall with a hammer. Now he's hanging some strong rings on the nails.

Frank What's Ann doing?

Ingrid She's bringing something interesting for Ron to drink. Now she's putting it down. He's asking for the drink and – Oh, no!

Frank What's happening?

Ingrid The ladder is breaking!

Frank Is Ron still standing on it?

Ingrid No, he's . . . he's hanging from the string. Oh, my goodness. He's holding onto the string by his fingers and laughing.

Frank Isn't Ann watching him?

Ingrid No. She's walking toward our house.

Frank You're joking!

Bell (*Ring! Ring! Ring!*)

Ingrid That's her ringing the bell!

Frank Well, I'm not answering it. I'm leaving.

2 Listen again and check your answers.

F Weak Pronunciation and Contraction of *be*

The verb *be* usually has a weak (unstressed) pronunciation in the middle of a sentence.

- Link the weak pronunciation of *be* to the word before it. The weak pronunciation of *are* (/ər/) sounds like the -er ending in *teacher*.
- After a pronoun, *be* is almost always contracted to '*m* (*I'm*), '*re* (*you're, we're, they're*), or '*s* (*he's, she's, it's*).

1 Listen and repeat.

What are they **do**ing?
They're **sing**ing.   I'm **sleep**ing.
You're **jok**ing!   He's **reach**ing for the **drink**.
We're **try**ing to **sleep**.   **What's hap**pening?

2 Talk about these pictures. Use falling intonation on the *Wh-* questions. Listen.

A What's **In**grid doing?

B She's looking out the **win**dow.

Ingrid

1. Ron King

2. Ron

3. Ann King

4. Ron

5. Ann

6. Frank

G Conversation Practice

1 Practice with a partner. Use the phrases below to make true sentences about yourself. Then listen to your partner's sentences.

Examples: I'm not wearing a ring.
I'm reading an interesting book.

1. wearing a ring
2. reading an interesting book
3. wearing something pink
4. taking a boring class
5. studying more than one language
6. planning a long trip
7. thinking of moving (to a new house or apartment)

2 Tell the class about the things that are true for both of you.

Examples: We're not wearing rings.
We're planning long trips.

H Spelling

The sound /ŋ/ is usually spelled with the letters *ng*. Before a /k/ or /g/ sound, /ŋ/ is spelled with the letter *n*. Add more examples below.

ng morning, ring, singing, wrong, _____
n before /k/: think, bank, uncle, _____
before /g/: finger, angry, English, language, hungry, longer, single

I Common Expressions

Listen and repeat these common expressions with the sound /ŋ/.

Good mor**ning**.
I'm hu**ng**ry.
Is somethi**ng** wro**ng**?

The phone is ri**ng**ing.
I've been waiti**ng** a lo**ng** time.
How lo**ng** have you been studyi**ng** E**ng**lish?

/l/ • light, fall

Weak Pronunciation and Contraction of *will*

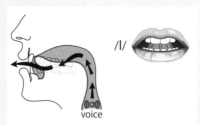

🎧 Put the tip of your tongue
   just behind your front teeth.
Use your voice.
To make the sound /l/, the air goes over the sides
   of your tongue and out of your mouth.
Listen and repeat: /l/.

A Word Pairs 1

🎧 **1** Listen to these word pairs.

	Sound 1: /n/	Sound 2: /l/	
	night	light	
	no	low	
	nine	line	
	connect	collect	
	snow	slow	

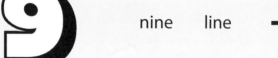

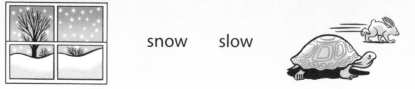

2 Listen again and repeat.

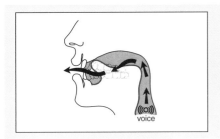

🎧 /l/ sounds a little different at the end
of a word or before a consonant.
As you say /l/, raise the back of your tongue
toward the roof of your mouth.
Listen and repeat: /l/.

B Word Pairs 2

🎧 **1** Listen to these word pairs.

Sound 1: /n/   **Sound 2: /l/**

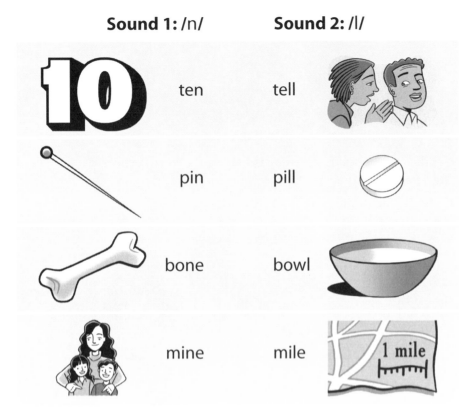

ten	tell	
pin	pill	
bone	bowl	
mine	mile	

2 Listen again and repeat.

C Test Yourself

🎧 **1** Listen and circle the word you hear.

1. no / low
2. night / light
3. connect / collect
4. ten / tell
5. bone / bowl
6. snow / slow

2 Listen to each sentence and circle the word you hear.

1. Is it (night / light) already?
2. Write it under the (nine / line).
3. I dropped a (pin / pill).
4. That's the dog's (bone / bowl).
5. There were (no / low) tables in the room.
6. He (connected / collected) the pieces.

3 Practice step **2** with a partner. Say each sentence, choosing a word from the word pair. Your partner should point to the word you say.

D Vocabulary

1 Listen and repeat these words with the sound /l/.

listen	a lot	college	eleven o'clock
look	late	relax	alarm clock
hello	early	usually	English class

2 The sound /l/ has a different, heavier sound at the end of a word or before a consonant. Listen and repeat.

call	help	trouble	almost always
well	cold	simple	fall asleep
cool	people	difficult	a glass of milk

E Dialog: Night owl

Solve Your Sleep Problems *is a radio show. People who have trouble sleeping can call and ask for help.*

1 Cover the dialog and listen. Then answer the questions.

1. What is Lilly's sleep problem? Check ✓ one.

   She falls asleep in her English class.
   She wakes up too early.
   She has trouble falling asleep.

2. What does Dr. Lopez suggest? Check ✓ all the true sentences.

Go to bed earlier.	Go to bed later.
Follow a regular schedule.	Sleep in a cool room.
Take sleeping pills.	Don't lie in bed looking at the clock.
Turn all the lights off.	Sleep in a comfortable bed.
Watch television in bed.	Don't watch television in bed.
Drink a glass of milk.	Don't eat a large meal late at night.

2 Listen again and read the dialog. Check your answers to step **1**.

Announcer	Welcome to *Solve Your Sleep Problems* with Dr. Sleep. Dr. Sleep's real name is Luisa Lopez, and she'll be taking calls from listeners. Do *you* have trouble sleeping? Here's our first caller now.
Dr. Lopez	Hello. Luisa Lopez here. Who's calling, please?
Lilly	Hello. My name is Lilly, and, uh, I'm a college student.
Dr. Lopez	Hello, Lilly. How well do *you* sleep?
Lilly	Not well at all. I have a *lot* of trouble falling asleep at night and then in the morning, I need two alarm clocks to wake me! I have an English class at eight o'clock, and I'm always late.
Dr. Lopez	When do you go to sleep, Lilly?
Lilly	I usually go to bed around, um, eleven o'clock.
Dr. Lopez	Maybe eleven o'clock is too early for you. We all have a biological clock that tells us when to sleep. Maybe *your* biological clock is telling you to go to bed later.
Lilly	Well, if I go to bed later, it still takes me a long time to fall asleep. How can I fall asleep more quickly?
Dr. Lopez	First of all, you should follow a regular schedule – always go to sleep and get up at the same time. Don't sleep late on the weekend.
Lilly	All right, I'll try.
Dr. Lopez	And do something relaxing before bed – no loud music or lively telephone calls.
Lilly	I hardly ever listen to loud music, so that'll be simple.
Dr. Lopez	Use your bed only for sleeping – not for watching television or reading.
Lilly	Well, that'll be difficult, because I always watch television in bed.
Dr. Lopez	And let's see, what else . . . Turn all the lights off. Keep your bedroom cool – but not cold. And last but not least, if you do have trouble falling asleep, don't look at the clock!
Lilly	My Mom always tells me to drink a glass of milk. Does that really help?
Dr. Lopez	Yes, it does. Milk has a chemical that helps people sleep. A glass of milk is an excellent idea.
Lilly	All right. I'll try all that.
Dr. Lopez	And one last thing: Maybe you should listen to your biological clock and look for a later English class!

F Weak Pronunciation and Contraction of *will*

Will is usually unstressed and has a weak pronunciation in the middle of a sentence.

- After a pronoun, *will* is usually contracted to *'ll*.
- In contractions with *will*, the vowel in the pronoun often sounds weaker or more relaxed. For example: *He'll* (sounds like *hill*) *call back*.

⌒ Listen and repeat.

I'll (/aɪl/) try.   She'll (/ʃɪl/) be taking calls.   That'll (ðætl) be more difficult.

Quiz: Night owl or early bird?

A night owl is a person who likes to stay up late. An early bird likes to get up early.

1 Work with a partner. For fun, take the quiz below. Complete each sentence with one of these words or phrases: *always / usually / occasionally / hardly ever / never.* Then listen to your partner's sentences.

Night Owl	Early Bird
1. I _____ have trouble falling asleep.	1. I _____ fall asleep in less than ten minutes.
2. I _____ need an alarm clock to wake up.	2. When I wake up, I _____ feel alert and cheerful.
3. When I wake up, I _____ feel sleepy and irritable.	3. I _____ get up when it starts to get light.
4. I _____ feel most alert in the early evening.	4. I _____ feel hungry early in the morning.
5. I _____ go to bed after twelve o'clock.	5. I _____ go to bed before eleven o'clock.

2 A night owl will answer *always* or *usually* to most of the questions on the left. An early bird will answer *always* or *usually* to most of the questions on the right. Does the quiz show that you are a night owl or an early bird? Do you agree?

H Spelling

The sound /l/ is spelled with the letter *l*. Add more examples below.

l   late, early, sleep, told, trouble, _____

ll   call, spell, really, excellent, _____

Careful: The letter *l* is sometimes silent when it comes before a consonant: talk, walk, half, could, should, would, yolk, calm, palm.

I Common Expressions

Listen and repeat these common expressions with the sound /l/.

Look out!	I'm leaving in a **little** while.
I'**ll call** you **later**.	I **fell** asleep.
I don't **feel well**.	**Lots** of **luck**!

/r/ • right

Stress in Long Words

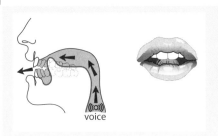

🎧 Turn the tip of your tongue up.
Do not touch the roof of your mouth with the tip
of your tongue.
Make your lips a little round.
Listen and repeat: /r/.

A Word Pairs

🎧 **1** Listen to these word pairs.

Sound 1: /l/	Sound 2: /r/
long	wrong
light	write
pilot	pirate
glass	grass
cloud	crowd

2 Listen again and repeat.

🎧 **1** Listen to the word pairs. Write *S* if the words are the same or *D* if the words are different.

1. _____   2. _____   3. _____   4. _____   5. _____   6. _____

🎧 **2** Listen to each sentence and circle the word you hear.

1. That sentence is (long / wrong).
2. Don't walk on the (glass / grass).
3. He was a famous (pilot / pirate).
4. I'm going to (collect / correct) the homework.
5. I couldn't see because of the (cloud / crowd).
6. Did you take the (light / right) suitcase?

3 Practice step **2** with a partner. Say each sentence, choosing a word from the word pair. Your partner should point to the word you say.

C Vocabulary

🎧 **1** Listen and repeat these words with the sound /r/.

reading	romantic	bright	remember
sorry	married	drawing	regards
writer	American	interesting	require
reporter	French	creative	photographer

🎧 **2** These words have both the sounds /r/ and /l/. Listen and repeat.

really	practical	responsibility	library
friendly	translator	congratulations	librarian
stressful	grandchildren	electrician	air traffic controller

D Dialog: Proud parents

Rose and Laura are old friends. They haven't seen each other in a long time.

🎧 **1** Cover the dialog and listen. Check ✓ the words in task C that Rose and Laura use to describe their children. Circle the jobs that their children have.

Rose Are your children grown up now, Laura?
Laura Oh, yes. Rachel is married and has three children.
Rose You're a grandmother? That's great! Congratulations!
Laura Thanks! But I don't see my grandchildren very much. Rachel and her family live in Paris.

Rose In Paris! Really?

Laura Yeah. Rachel is a reporter for an American newspaper. Her husband is a French photographer. They met when they were reporting on the same story.

Rose How romantic! And what about Grace? Is she married, too? She was such a bright girl – always reading.

Laura No, she isn't married, but she has a boyfriend. And she still reads a lot. She's a librarian at the public library. So, what about your children?

Rose Do you remember Roger?

Laura Of course, I remember Roger. Is he in college?

Rose Oh, no. He graduated. Right now he's working as a translator, but what he really wants to do is write.

Laura That's not surprising. He was a very creative little boy – always drawing or writing stories.

Rose You're right – he'd like a job with more creativity.

Laura And what about Brian? He was more practical, if I remember correctly – less of a dreamer.

Rose Brian is an air traffic controller in Florida.

Laura Really? Very interesting.

Rose Yeah, it's an interesting job – but stressful.

Laura Does his job require a lot of travel?

Rose Not really. But he has a lot of responsibility. I'm sorry, Laura, I have to run now. I'm late for my train. But I'm really glad I ran into you.

Laura Great to see you, too, Rose. Give my regards to everybody!

2 Listen again and read the dialog. Check your answers to step **1**.

E Stress in Long Words

Long words are often built by adding an ending to a shorter word.

- When an ending is added to a word, often the stressed syllable in the word does not change. Endings that do not usually change the stress include *-er, -or, -ful, -ing,* and *-ly.*
- But some endings do change the stressed syllable in a word. When the endings *-ian, -ic, -ical, -ion,* and *-ity* are added to a word, the strong stress usually moves to the syllable just before the ending.

1 The stressed syllable stays the same when we add these endings. Listen and repeat.

re**port** + -er = re**port**er
trans**late** + -or = **trans**lator
interest + -ing = **in**teresting

beauty + -ful = **beau**tiful
probable + -ly = **prob**ably

2 Stress moves to the syllable just before the ending in these words. Listen and repeat.

library + -ian = li**brar**ian   **po**litics + -ical = po**lit**ical

e**lec**tric + -ian = elec**tric**ian   con**grat**ulate + -ions = congratu**la**tions

romance + -ic = ro**man**tic   re**spon**sible + -ity = responsi**bil**ity

3 Try these. Underline the stressed syllable in each word.

friendly	creativity	politician
stressful	opportunity	artistic
promotion	practical	surprising

F Discussion

1 Practice in a group of two or three people. Talk about the things that are most important to you in a job. Choose three of the items below to complete this sentence:

I'd like a job that . . .

is interesting	has friendly people
isn't very stressful	has opportunities for promotion
requires creativity	requires working with a group
has a lot of responsibility	requires working alone
has flexible hours	pays very well
requires problem-solving	requires a lot of writing
requires travel	doesn't require a lot of writing

2 After each person has completed the sentence, discuss the job each person would probably like to have.

G Spelling

The sound /r/ is usually spelled with the letter *r*. Add more examples below.

r   right, repeat, really, _____

rr   sorry, tomorrow, married, correct

Other spellings: <u>wr</u>ong, <u>wr</u>ite, <u>rh</u>ythm, <u>rh</u>yme

H Common Expressions

Listen and repeat these common expressions with the sound /r/.

Great!	**R**elax!
Try it.	Are you **r**eady?
All **r**ight.	I'm **r**eally so**rr**y.

UNIT 49

/r/ • after vowels

Intonation in Polite Questions

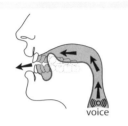

voice

🎧 To say the sound /r/ after a vowel, curl the tip of your tongue up.
Do not touch the roof of your mouth with the tip of your tongue.
Listen and repeat: /r/.

A Word Pairs

🎧 **1** Listen to these word pairs.

Sound 1: /l/	**Sound 2: /r/**
heel	hear
pail	pear
fall	four
file	fire
towel	tower

2 Listen again and repeat.

B Test Yourself

🎧 **1** Listen and circle the word you hear.

1. fall / four   3. file / fire   5. towel / tower

2. heel / hear   4. pail / pear   6. pool / poor

🎧 **2** Listen to each sentence and circle the word you hear.

1. Put this paper in the (file / fire).

2. I put the (pail / pear) in the kitchen.

3. (Fall / Four) is the best time to go there.

4. Did you find the (towel / tower)?

5. You shouldn't (feel / fear) it.

6. We need more money for the (pool / poor).

3 Practice step **2** with a partner. Say each sentence, choosing a word from the word pair. Your partner should point to the word you say.

C Vocabulary

1 Work with a partner. Write each word in the correct column in the table below.

hear	chair	first	before	clerk
four	start	morning	upstairs	clear
far	here	near	worse	aren't
thirty	there	large	where	toward

1: /ɪr/	2: /ɛr/	3: /ɑr/	4: /ər/	5: /ɔr/
hear	chair	far	thirty	four

🎧 **2** Listen. Repeat the words and check your answers.

D Dialog: At the airport

Mary and Aaron are at the airport. Their flight has been delayed.

1 Work with a partner. Read the dialog on the next page. Fill in the blanks with words from task C.

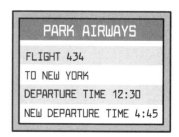

```
PARK AIRWAYS
FLIGHT 434
TO NEW YORK
DEPARTURE TIME 12:30
NEW DEPARTURE TIME 4:45
```

Announcement Good _____morning_____. Passengers on Park Airways flight 434, scheduled to depart for New York at 12:30, there will be a short delay. That flight will now depart at 4:45. Passengers should remain here at the airport. We're sorry . . .

Aaron Did you hear that? It wasn't very _____.

Mary There's going to be a short delay. We _____ leaving until a quarter to five.

Aaron SHORT delay?! That's more than _____ hours!

Mary Well, I'm thirsty. Do you know if there's a coffee bar here?

Aaron I'm not sure. Oh, there's an airline clerk. Ask her.

Mary (*to the airline clerk*) Pardon me, is _____ a coffee bar here?

Airline clerk A coffee bar? No, sorry. This isn't a very _____ airport. But there's a cafeteria _____, near the security check.

Mary Thanks.
(*to Aaron*) I'm going upstairs. Coming, dear?

Aaron No. I'm tired. I'm going to find a comfortable _____ and stay here. (*to the airline clerk*) Where's the nearest restroom?

Airline clerk Right over there, _____ gate 14.

Aaron Is there a problem with the airplane?

Airline clerk Oh, no, sir. There's a storm moving toward here, and the weather forecast says it will get _____ before it gets better. But it should clear up in a couple of hours.

Aaron Are you sure?

Airline clerk Oh, yes, sir. Flight 434 will be the _____ plane to leave after the storm. Our departure time is 4:45. We'll start boarding at quarter after four.

🎧 **2** Listen to the dialog and check your answers.

E Intonation in Polite Questions

To make a question sound polite, the intonation often starts high, jumps down on the stressed syllable of the most important word, and then rises at the end of the question.

- This intonation can be used for both *Yes / No* and *Wh-* questions.
- This intonation is often used when asking a stranger a question.

🎧 Listen and repeat.

Is there a **cof**fee bar here?   Where's the nearest **rest**room?

F Conversation Practice

Practice in a group of three or four people. Take turns asking for directions to places in your town or neighborhood. Ask about places like the ones below. Listen to these examples:

A **Par**don me. Is there a **book**store near here?

B **Yes**. There's a bookstore on the **cor**ner.

A Where's the nearest **tour**ist office?

B **Sor**ry, I'm really not **sure**.

a **park**	a **book**store	a **hair**dresser	a **flor**ist
the **air**port	a **hard**ware store	a **farm**er's market	a cafe**ter**ia
a **tour**ist office	a de**part**ment store	a **li**brary	

G Spelling

The sound /ɪr/ is usually spelled with the letters *ear, eer,* or *er.*

ear near, hear, clear
eer cheerful, deer
er cafeteria, serious, experience

Other spellings: h<u>ere</u>, we'<u>re</u>, cash<u>ier</u>

The sound /ɛr/ is usually spelled with the letters *air* or *are.*

air air, chair, hair, upstairs
are care, scared, compare

Other spellings: w<u>ear</u>, p<u>ear</u>, wh<u>ere</u>, th<u>ere</u>, th<u>eir</u>, p<u>ar</u>ent, <u>are</u>a

The sound /ʊr/ is usually spelled with the letters *ure* or *ur.*

ure sure, pure
ur curious, plural

Other spelling: p<u>oor</u>

For the sound /ɑr/, /ɔr/, and /ər/, see Units 10, 11, and 21.

H Common Expressions

Listen and repeat these common expressions with the sound /r/ after vowels.

Take **care**!	Are you **sure**?
Is it n**ear** h**ere**?	Wh**ere** are you from?
How **far** is it from h**ere**?	Wh**ere** were you b**orn**?

Review

UNIT 50 /m/, /n/, /ŋ/, /l/, and /r/

A Test Yourself

🎧 Listen and circle the word you hear. You can use a dictionary if you like, but you don't have to understand every word to do this.

1. some / sun / sung
2. ram / ran / rang
3. clam / clan / clang
4. rum / run / rung
5. night / light / right
6. connect / collect / correct

7. wait / late / rate
8. wide / lied / ride
9. he's / heels / hears
10. sought / salt / sort
11 two's / tools / tours
12. wide / wild / wired

B Intonation

🎧 Listen. Circle the question that shows the intonation you hear. Then choose the most likely explanation for the intonation. The speaker is probably:

a. talking to someone they know.
b. asking someone to repeat.
c. asking a stranger for information.
Write *a*, *b*, or *c* in the blank.

1. Where's the nearest **bank**?   ___b___

   (Where's) the nearest bank?

   Where's the nearest **bank**?

2. When does the **plane** leave?   _____

   When does the plane leave?

   When does the **plane** leave?

3. What time does the **li**brary close?   _____

   What time does the **li**brary close?

   What time does the **li**brary close?

4. Where can I find a **rest**room? _____

Where can I find a restroom?

Where can I find a **rest**room?

5. What **time** is it? _____

What time is it?

What **time** is it?

6. When does the **plane** leave? _____

When does the plane leave?

When does the **plane** leave?

7. Where's the nearest **bank**? _____

Where's the nearest bank?

Where's the nearest **bank**?

8. What **time** is it? _____

What time is it?

What **time** is it?

C Puzzle: Which word doesn't belong?

Circle the word in each line that does not have the same stress pattern as the others.

1. require	connect	asleep	(oven)
2. bedroom	myself	sometimes	midnight
3. remember	tomorrow	probably	apartment
4. important	forbidden	romantic	practical
5. relaxing	interesting	happening	listening
6. responsible	comfortable	photographer	librarian